lemmings don't leap

180 myths, misconceptions and urban legends exploded

Edwin Moore

Chambers

CHAMBERS
An imprint of Chambers Harrap Publishers Ltd
7 Hopetoun Crescent
Edinburgh, EH7 4AY

www.chambers.co.uk

First published by Chambers Harrap Publishers Ltd 2006
Reprinted 2006

A CIP catalogue record for this book is available from the British Library.

ISBN-13 978 0550 10293 5
ISBN-10 0550 10293 0

Editor: Liam Rodger
Publishing Manager: Patrick White
Prepress Controller: David Reid, Heather Macpherson
Prepress: Nadia Cornuau

Designed and typeset by Chambers Harrap Publishers Ltd, Edinburgh
Printed and bound by Clays Ltd, St Ives plc

Contents

Contents

Music and Musicians

Screen, Stage and TV

USA, Past and Present

Contents

Writers, Language and Writing

History – Ancient and Medieval

History – Renaissance to 19th Century

Contents

History – 20th Century

The Mythical and the Paranormal

Ugly Rumours

Religion

Introduction

I once had a conversation with a man in a pub. He was clutching a video of *The Wild Bunch*, and I mentioned that the Peckinpah 'Director's cut' was a waste of celluloid (see **Director's cuts are not the definitive version**); not only did he not flee, he knew what I was talking about and agreed with me. We chatted some more and (as he will) Errol Flynn came up. I said it was a shame he didn't have a decent script when playing Custer in *They Died with Their Boots On*, and - joy of joy - the man pulled from his briefcase a copy of *Greasy Grass* magazine (the name comes, of course, from what the Lakota called their victory over Custer: 'the Greasy Grass fight' – a fitting title for a publication devoted to the Little Big Horn battle). I fell upon it with rapture: in those pre-web days, children, such mags were devoured by seekers after arcane truths.

The odd thing is, though, the more the Greasy Grass fight has been studied the more opaque it becomes. A victory - however temporary - for the oppressed? Well yes, except the Pawnee, Crow and other Native Americans saw the Lakota as imperial oppressors - they didn't fight for the whites because they liked them, they fought because their existence was at stake. We have lots of Native American eye-witnesses, don't we? We do, but the witnesses all seem to have been present at different battles (see **Oral history can be bunk**).

'Facts are chiels that winna ding', said Burns ('facts cannot be gainsaid'), how very true (see, by the way, **Robert Burns wanted to be a slave overseer**). The store of indisputable facts about Greasy Grass has been added to recently. Studies of the bones of the 7th Cavalry troopers demonstrate convincingly that these men were in a bad way to begin with, malnourished and with unhealed wounds – in fact quite unlike the strapping fellows we see in John Ford westerns, like that archetypal screen Irishman, Victor McLaglen. But did you know that this 'Irishman' was the best boxer in the British Army and ruled Baghdad in 1918? Well, you do now (see **Victor McLaglen was a British officer and not an Irish sergeant**).

Sometimes - alas - you just can't get the final answers (see **The Great**

Library of Alexandria was not destroyed by the Arabs). But some of life's awkward questions can be answered. Did President Kennedy really say 'I am a doughnut' to a cheering crowd of Berliners? Hitler did storm out of the Berlin Olympics after Jesse Owens won a gold medal, didn't he? Wasn't it terrible that Vietnam veterans got spat on when they came home? Is the back garden safe for Tiddles with those foxes kicking about? Didn't Brando look cool on that Harley-Davidson in *The Wild One*? Read on and learn, is all I will say for the present…

Here is the truth behind 180 of life's myths, misconceptions and urban legends (with an occasional inspirational and unexpected truth thrown in). As an extra, the book has scattered through it a few dozen panels (headed 'Not in so many words') which correct some widely repeated misquotations and bogusly-attributed sayings. The number of 'things we know that ain't so' is large and growing, but this, at any rate, is a start at setting the record straight.

The trouble with a smart-arse book like this, of course, is that the author, who can make no claims to infallibility, might unwittingly be spreading a few tall tales himself. Am I really sure that **You may share more DNA with a chimp than an African elephant does with an Asian elephant**? I'm no expert on DNA after all, but that's what it looks like the experts are saying - at this time.

I have good reason to be cautious, having once had to take the flak for a Scottish 'fact' book that omitted Bannockburn from a list of Scottish battles - and oh dear, there's nothing quite so scary as the Scottish media on the warpath. I was shouted at in *The Scotsman*, *The Sun*, the *Daily Record* and *The Herald*, and was given a hard time live on Radio Scotland. I learned the hard way how difficult it is to respond sensibly to questions like 'why have you insulted the Scottish nation?' (how *do* you 'insult a nation?').

This book would certainly have been much more insultable were it not for a few sharp-eyed friends: my thanks are especially due to Alice Goldie for correcting my science and bad taste; to Merlin Holland for clearing up the details around his grandfather's alleged transvestism (see **Oscar Wilde was not photographed in drag**); to George MacDonald Fraser for being so good to steal from (in fact and fiction); and to Mike Munro, who saved me from putting Vivien Leigh into Hitchcock's shower instead of Janet Leigh (and what a movie that would have been! - see **Hitchcock did direct the shower scene in *Psycho***). But my greatest debt is to my editor Liam Rodger, who has, with great tact, saved me from several appalling errors, and has also made loads of improvements to the text.

Any remaining mistakes herein are all mine. Several websites and books laugh at the movie *Casablanca* for having fog at the end when - actually - this is perfectly common in North African ports (see **Ronald Reagan was not the original choice for Rick in *Casablanca***), so some of my smugness may alas be equally unmerited. Do feel free to write in with your suggestions and corrections, which will be acknowledged in future editions. But please… don't gloat!

Dedication

This book is for my mother, of whom life asked many hard questions. A nurse during WWII and a cleaner for over 40 years after, she walked her own path without complaint. Though always fastidious, she cleaned up the sick and dying when young; though always a monarchist, she upstaged the Queen when old (at the Queen's own party); and though always poor, she kept her children clothed and fed and housed.

The Natural World

Lemmings do not leap off cliffs

The fable of suicidal lemmings is remarkably persistent. Every four years (or so), it is said, Arctic-dwelling lemmings get into a mass panic and start migrating as their population expands; the deluded wee beasts then end up tumbling over cliffs into the sea in their mad dash for territory.

There is a tiny grain of truth here in that Scandinavian lemmings will migrate when their numbers dramatically increase, but lemming populations expand and contract just as other rodent populations do. Accidents occur, and lemmings will fall off heights and into water as any other animal would do under pressure, but there is no avalanche of lemmings into the North Sea (or anywhere else). When the population reaches the 'boom' stage of its cycle, the animals suffer heavy predation from stoats, snowy owls and other predators, which results in an equally dramatic fall in numbers.

Unusually for a myth of this kind, its creation can be precisely dated, and its creator was Walt Disney Studios. In 1958, Disney issued a 'documentary' called *White Wilderness*, which included a sequence of lemmings jumping over a cliff into the sea. The sequence looks convincing but is totally manufactured. The lemming scenes were filmed in Alberta and as lemmings don't live there, they had to be brought in from Manitoba. They were then filmed on a turntable to make them look like a suitably vast migrating horde before being taken to a cliff and herded over the edge into a river (supposedly the sea – Alberta doesn't actually have a coastline).

It is not known whether Disney himself knew how the film crew had staged this sorry sequence.

Dinosaurs did not rule the earth (at least not the bits near water)

We can all picture dinosaurs 'ruling' the earth. This is partly due to bad Hollywood movies of course, but also because we've unquestioningly absorbed the notion that dinosaurs were the biggest and meanest creatures of their time – the period of about 170 million years from the Triassic to the Cretaceous. We may also have a vague notion of brave little mammals (our ancestors) scurrying about under the feet of the giants, maybe even stealing their eggs. But there is one beast, still with us today, that lived then and gave even the biggest, baddest dinosaurs serious trouble.

Crocodiles are the last of the 'archosaurs', the ancient reptiles. They have become smaller over the millennia, the two biggest modern species being the Nile and the larger saltwater crocs (which can measure more than 20 feet), but in the past they grew to truly enormous sizes.

Crocodiles live on both land and in water, and hunt where the two environments meet. They are the ultimate ambush predator, and they strike fast when a meal walks within lunging reach. Crocodilian hunting strategy has been so successful that it has not changed for millions of years. A large carnosaur such as T Rex measured 30-40 feet from head to tail. But that 40 feet of menace had to go down to the river to drink, and in the rivers were the big crocs – 30 to 50 ft long. An attack by one of those animals launching itself out of the water must have been like being hit by a train with teeth. We know the crocs of North America ate carnosaurs: the gnawed bones of Albertosaurs have been found in Georgia, where the large crocs lived in swampy environments.

Crocodiles worked out early the best way of doing what they do, and they have had no need to evolve. They ate dinosaurs, eat us, and will no doubt still be around to eat what comes after us.

It is unlikely that we co-exist with carnivorous sharks longer than Routemaster buses

In his first encounter with the great white shark in the novel *Jaws* (1974), the shark expert Hooper exclaims 'Megalodon!' and rhapsodizes about the possibility of the fish being a modern version of that huge prehistoric creature – a species of shark that lived around 15 million years ago and grew to 40-50 feet long (the Routemaster bus was 30 feet long). This possibility has found its way into Steve Alten's charmingly titled 'Meg' series of novels, such as *The Trench* (1999), which posits the existence of surviving megalodons in the Mariana Trench.

'Megalodon' means 'great tooth' and it was certainly a fearsome beast. Some enthusiasts used to reckon the creature reached 100 feet but this is very likely many yards too far. It certainly grew to over 50 feet and that is a monstrous size for a carnivorous fish. Indeed, from the size of the teeth – they have been found up to 7 inches long – the upper length of megalodon may have approached 70 feet. There are of course sharks of comparable size still living: whale sharks can get to about 50 feet in length and basking sharks are not far behind. But if you encountered either of these, the most you would suffer is a sore bump or a bad scrape from a fin. An ocean encounter with a living megalodon would be a lot more painful (but not for long).

We don't actually know what megalodon (*Carcharodon megalodon*) looked like. It is generally portrayed as a giant version of a great white shark (*Carcharodon carcharias*) as in the BBC series *The Seven Deadliest Seas*, but although the teeth do look remarkably similar, it is entirely possible that the great white does not in fact descend from megalodon and indeed looks nothing like it.

What are the chances of encountering a megalodon? A fish that was believed to have become extinct millions of years ago, the coelacanth, was rediscovered in 1938, and a large new species of shark, megamouth, was only found in 1976. Megamouth (which is likely to be rare) seems to be a plankton feeder and inhabits the deeps. But megalodon was a very large carnivore, and large carnivores tend to make their presence felt in their ecosystems (giant squids are rare but we've known of their existence for a long time). The fictional great white shark in *Jaws* is 25 feet long, whereas the accepted record length for the species is 21 feet (the shark in *Jaws* is also male, but large whites are almost always females). Shark length estimates, as with other large predators, always err on the large side. A 16-ft white shark is a simply huge creature, and will get bigger in the memory, and if there were carnivorous sharks over 50 foot long about it seems probable that at least one would have been taken as a specimen by now. The consensus is that megalodon was a highly visible coastal hunter, not a deep-water creature, like Alten's 'Meg'.

It was formerly believed that megalodon existed until about 40,000 years ago – see *Great White Shark* (1991) by Ellis and McCosker – but this is now seen as very unlikely. The best current guess is that this monster fish disappeared at the end of the Pliocene, about 1.5 million years ago, a fair bit before modern humans came along, and that it isn't coming back (at least not outside the covers of a novel).

➤ *See also* **The deadliest thing about the sand tiger shark is not its bite...**

The Coriolis Effect does not work for toilets

The Coriolis Effect is the inertial force that deflects an object moving above the earth – rightward in the Northern hemisphere and leftward in the Southern hemisphere.

The concept is finely illustrated in an episode of *The Simpsons*, 'Bart vs Australia'. Lisa explains to Bart that this is why in toilets in the Northern hemisphere (eg America) water drains anti-clockwise whereas in the Southern hemisphere water drains the other way.

Bart won't accept this and phones up various people in the Southern hemisphere to see how their toilets drain, and in the process creates a diplomatic incident with Australia. This results in the Simpson family travelling to Australia so Bart can apologise in person. In the American embassy, it is touchingly revealed that 'to combat homesickness' a special device has been installed in the toilets to make them swirl 'the correct American way'.

Unfortunately, even Lisa Simpson gets it wrong sometimes. Australian toilets flush in the same direction that all toilets in the world do. The Coriolis force can and does influence the movement of large bodies of water or air masses in the atmosphere, but has a negligible effect on the tiny quantities of water in a sink or toilet bowl. In the latter the shape of the receptacles and the way water is poured into them are what determine the direction of flow.

The myth of the rotating water reached its height (or depth) in an episode of Michael Palin's documentary series *Pole to Pole*, where Palin is on the equator in a Kenyan town and is given a demonstration of the Coriolos Effect in operation on a pan of water, as a man carries the pan from one side of the equator to the other. Ludicrously, at one point the man stands directly on the equator and Palin says: 'So, now we are right on the equator, and as we drain the water, you'll see there will be no rotation. It just drains straight down. And that's how we prove that we are right on the equator.'

In fact, the entire performance is just that, a show put on for tourists.

The deadliest thing about the sand tiger shark is not its bite...

The sand tiger shark (*Carcharias taurus*) belongs to the order of mackerel sharks, and is a quite distinct species from the tiger shark proper. The latter is most definitely a threat to people within its range, not just because it is pretty big, but also because it has evolved to try to catch and eat more or less anything (the largest carnivorous shark of them all, the great white, has evolved to have a great preference for seals). Sand tigers, however, are regarded by most authorities as basically harmless to humans (though attacks have apparently been recorded in American waters).

The sand tiger shark is a very popular choice with owners of marine shows and large aquariums. These sharks seem easy to please, do well in captivity and cohabit with fish they would normally prey on as long as they are regularly fed, and they can live up to 10 years in captivity (most other big sharks tend to die more quickly in aquariums).

Their greatest attraction is undoubtedly that they are good at looking fearsome, cruising along past the glass with their sticky-out teeth. The teeth look wonderfully menacing but are in fact adapted to catch small fish and crabs. Even 10-ft sand tiger sharks will invariably avoid humans, but they do have a rather unsettling special skill. The normal choice of an animal challenged by another animal is 'fight or flight': the sand tiger adds another option beginning with 'f': flatulence.

The sand tiger is not one of the more energetic sharks and when not hunting it seems to like hanging about in groups doing very little, much like a bored teenager. The special skill they have is that they go to the surface periodically and gulp in surface water; the water is then held in the stomach, and the shark can fart it out to adjust its position in the water, thereby conserving energy, and when a potentially threatening organism appears the shark farts in its general direction, which has the double advantage of moving the shark away from the potential predator and is quite disconcerting for any nearby creature, predator or not.

➤ *See also* **It is unlikely that we co-exist with carnivorous sharks longer than Routemaster buses.**

Goldfish do have memories

The common misconception that goldfish do not have much of a memory is the subject of many cartoons. For example, one fish says to the other occupant of their tiny bowl: 'Do you come here often?'...

The goldfish memory span is commonly said to be three seconds long. As this is the average time it takes to swim round the bowl, each new three-second vista forms, supposedly, an entirely new experience. However, a moment's thought should lead one to the conclusion that a vertebrate which could not retain memories beyond three seconds is one unlikely to survive as a pampered pond resident, never mind in the wild. In fact, when goldfish are introduced into foreign environments such as canals, it is often the indigenous species that get squeezed out.

The myth is an especially odd one, given that goldfish are possibly the oldest and most observed of domesticated fish. When fed only at set times, they will expect to be fed at that time, and will even quickly adapt to hand-feeding. Further, goldfish can learn to prompt the feeding by pressing on a lever, as has been demonstrated by research by Dr Phil Gee of Plymouth University. As Dr Gee reports: 'Activity around the lever increased enormously just before the set hour when their food was dispensed. But then if no food came out, they stopped pressing the lever when the hour was up. It shows that they are probably able to adapt to changes in their circumstances, like any other small animals and birds.'

➤ *See also* **Fish do feel pain.**

Not in so many words

"Alas, poor Yorick. I knew him well." What Hamlet actually says is rather more wistful: "Alas, poor Yorick. I knew him, Horatio – a fellow of infinite jest, of most excellent fancy."

Black widow spiders never (well hardly ever...) eat their mates

The hapless fly in Don Marquis's poem 'a spider and a fly' tries to argue that flies benefit all of nature by spreading diseases that kill off the world's curse, humans. The spider observes that this may be true, while cutting off a fly sirloin, but it is a strictly utilitarian point of no consequence to artists such as himself.

Some spiders may kill us – and in very painful ways – but without them the insects would have a great time with us (spiders are of course arachnids and not insects). The biggest and hairiest spiders – tarantulas – can give us sore bites but are rarely deadly. Black widow and recluse spiders can (also rarely) give bites which lead to horrible deaths though their main business is generally not with us, but with their prey and predators (they have many of both).

Misconceptions about spiders abound, a common one being that female black widows always eat their mates. In fact this hardly ever happens in the wild. As long as the male – who is smaller and non-poisonous – vibrates the web in the correct manner before approaching the female, he is safe enough. Few male black widows break the rules of mating, at least not more than once.

The black widow, as Gordon Grice points out in his rather unnerving book *The Red Hourglass* (1998), has lots of myths attached to it.

It eats its mate, it comes flooding in from Asia, it can lurk in bouffant hairdos, it is even, according to another book, *Black Widow: America's Most Poisonous Spider* (1945), aligned with the communist menace: '[the] deadliest communists are like the black widow spider; they conceal their red underneath'. As Grice points out, referring to this passage, we thus 'project our archetypal terrors onto the widow'.

Polar bears are black

Judging from appearance, polar bears are about as white as animals can get. But appearances can be deceptive: polar bears are actually black.

Polar bear skin is black. The black skin allows the animal to soak up heat from the sun, and the skin is covered in hollow, translucent hairs that disperse light. Polar bears are white in the same way that clouds are white, ie there is no pigment in the hairs, and it is the reflection and scattering of light that gives the appearance of whiteness. The noses (and paws) are uncovered and it is sometimes claimed, as in the *Guinness Book of Animal Facts and Feats*, that a polar bear will cover its nose with its paw when stalking seals, though no one seems to have actually seen this happen. They cover their noses while sleeping, as do other mammals.

In some zoos, such as Singapore, polar bears have been observed to turn green, the result, apparently, of hot weather causing algae growth within the hollow hairs. Polar bears are the world's largest land carnivores, their only rival being Kodiak bears. Large polar bears can weigh 1,400 lb and stand over 9 ft tall. The largest on record weighed in at a colossal 2,200 lb and was over 12 ft tall, about as formidable a mammalian carnivore as has ever lived. Even eating one would be risky: polar bear liver is highly toxic to other carnivores as it has a high concentration of vitamin A.

Implausible as it seems, there are indeed bears which are truly white, and they are *black* bears: a variant of the black bear found in western Canada called the Kermode (or Spirit) bear (first described in 1905) is indeed coloured white.

Fish do feel pain

This is an issue of some consequence to fish of course, but also to people who keep fish as pets, who farm them or who hunt them. If fish do feel pain, then can angling (or fish farms) be justified?

Up until recent times, it has been assumed that fish do not feel pain, and it has even been argued that no animal feels pain. The French philosopher Descartes went so far as to claim that animals were simply cleverly designed automata that mimicked pain, and that their apparently distressed reactions to torment were of no more significance than the ticking of a clock. The more down-to-earth English philosopher Jeremy Bentham had a fine and deadly riposte to this kind of sophistical reasoning: 'The question is not, Can they reason nor Can they talk, but, Can they suffer?' Science has recently caught up with philosophy and established beyond any reasonable doubt that fish do indeed feel pain and can suffer.

The evidence is in a much-pondered Royal Society paper of 2003 that provides 'the first conclusive evidence indicating pain perception in fish'. The scientists involved applied 'noxious' substances to the nervous system receptors of rainbow trout and produced reactions that fulfilled 'the criteria for animal pain'.

This confirms what most of us actually believe according to the evidence of our eyes: fish are sentient creatures. A fish wriggling on a hook displays pretty much identical behaviour to that displayed by a human impaled on a spike, and science now confirms that this is not mere Cartesian mimicry. What we do with this knowledge is, of course, another matter.

➤ *See also* **Goldfish do have memories.**

Wild animals do attack people

One of the great propaganda successes of the environmental movement in the 20th century was the rehabilitation of large predators, particularly in the USA. Cougars, alligators and bears, once hunted to the brink of extinction, were encouraged to flourish. Much play was made of how humans were a mortal danger to these magnificent killers. In this telling of the story, we were certainly the bad guys.

Humans have been hunting North America's megafauna since the Pleistocene, as soon as the 'Clovis' Indians began arriving around 10,000 years BC, during a period of great climate change. These first Americans learned to respect and live with the animals that they found, such as the large bears of the woods. Bears were hunted, of course, but hunted with great care. Killing a large and often bad-tempered omnivore possessing huge teeth and claws is an energy-expending business at best and life-threatening at worst. It wasn't because of any mystical relationship that Indians didn't mess with bears; they didn't mess with bears because to do so is very stupid.

Perhaps influenced by 1960s thinking about benign and endangered predators, a man called Treadwell spent 12 summers living with grizzlies in the Alaskan wilderness with his girlfriend. He loved the bears, and gave them names such as Mr Chocolate and Aunt Melissa. He said he would give his life for the bears. Then one day he did. A grizzly ate him and his girlfriend. The grizzly was shot, and German film-maker Werner Herzog made a characteristic nutter-against-the-world film about it all, called *Grizzly Man* (2005). The film includes an interview with an Indian saying that Treadwell had 'crossed the boundary we've lived with'.

At least Treadwell had to go out into the wilderness to find his grisly end. Cougars were commonly said to be terribly shy of humans, and there were few records of attacks – they didn't even bother livestock so nervy were they of human settlement. California saw an attack in 1890 and one in 1909. Thereafter there was nothing until 1986, but they now average one a year, including one in a San Diego car park. There is now the inevitable support group for attack survivors, called CLAW (Californian Lion Awareness).

Alligators have killed very few Americans, but there is no doubt that attacks are increasing. Attacks by sharks also increased quite dramatically on America's east coast by the beginning of the 21st century. The temptation to think nature is trying to tell America something should be resisted; all it means is that more unwary people in the proximity of more large animals inevitably means more trouble.

➤ *See also **Dolphins are not as friendly as their smiles suggest.***

Homosexual acts are not unnatural

A popular motif in Valentine's Day cards is a shot of two giraffes apparently 'necking'. In fact, the two giraffes will almost certainly be male and about to fight each other for dominance. But male giraffes don't only fight each other – they also have sex with each other.

Same-sex activity has presumably always been present in nature, but it has only recently begun to be recorded. The explosion of interest in natural history in 18th-century England – an interest which meant that the average educated person was better prepared to accept Darwin's Theory of Evolution than we tend to assume – means that same-sex behaviour must have been frequently observed, yet went completely unrecorded. According to the great majority of Victorian moralists, homosexual acts among humans were 'acts against nature'. We now know for certain that such a view is wrong thanks to the willingness of observers to record scientifically what has always – in reality – been there.

Most so-called 'higher' animals, such as dolphins, engage in homosexual activity, though it is found in 'lower' animals also, such as snails. Homosexual relationships are common among primates such as chimps, and macaques – and of course humans. As much as a third of macaque sexual activity is between females, though bonobo chimps are the primate group with the largest amount of recorded homosexual activity: indeed, the majority of bonobo sexual activity is same-sex.

A monogamous male-female partnership seems to be a minority relationship in the animal kingdom. Horse breeders have long known that stallions – that potent symbol of male sexuality – are prone to bisexuality. Such bisexual behaviour is common in birds, notably penguins. The movie *The March of the Penguins* (2005) was famously (and bizarrely) seen as a celebration of monogamous male-female sexuality in the USA, yet many stable penguin pairs are actually same-sex.

It used to be argued that same-sex activity could not exist as it had no apparent evolutionary advantage, but it now turns out to be so common that the question is now what the advantage (or advantages) might be, and this has become a prolific field of study.

11

'Faux' fur is often real fur

Those who choose to wear fur see it as a simple matter of choice and view opponents of fur as rather hypocritical, as many will happily wear leather shoes and eat meat. A fair point, except that it does not take into account how the bulk of the world's fur is produced. There is more than enough evidence to show that animals, including cats and dogs, are skinned alive for their fur in China. This is because it saves time: the skinners (who work in groups) are generally on piece rates and killing an animal without damaging the skin takes both skill and time. The skinned animals obviously die very unpleasant deaths.

The fur is sold on cheaply to wholesalers who sell it on to manufacturers, including some of the world's top fashion houses. In 2004, £7 million worth of dog and cat fur was reportedly brought into the UK. Some manufacturers use made-up names to describe the fur they use, such as 'Asian jackal' for dog, or 'goyangi' for cat, though most don't bother.

Fake fur could be a useful alternative, though it is an alternative disliked by most vegetarians and vegans, who have a problem with the fact that a sham fur can be seen as paying tribute to the real article. But there is a further problem, which is that real fur (and leather) is now so cheap on the world market that it can be cheaper to produce a garment labelled as faux-fur which is actually made of the real thing – and you will be very unlikely to track down the true provenance. Company buyers keep their jobs by getting good supplies cheaply, and it has never been easier to get quality furs cheaply. It really should be the companies who ensure that buyers keep to ethical guidelines on animal welfare, but this is unlikely to happen without consumer pressure – which is as yet largely absent.

Iceland is green and Greenland is ice

Iceland and Greenland are two lands linked by some shared culture and a huge misunderstanding in that both are misnamed: Iceland is (or could be) green, while Greenland is most definitely icy, as the old missionary hymn says in stunningly non-PC language:

From Greenland's icy mountains, from India's coral strand,
Where Afric's sunny fountains roll down their golden sand;
From many an ancient river, from many a palmy plain,
They call us to deliver their land from error's chain.

It is occasionally suggested the names were swapped, presumably at the instigation of the Icelanders, but this is untrue. Although there were human settlers on Greenland around 2,000 years ago, the island seems to have been empty of people when the Icelanders arrived at the end of the 10th century. The Icelandic settlers were later joined by migrating Inuit (*see **The Inuit do not have hundreds of words for snow***). The settlers were led by the exiled desperado Erik the Red and his clan, who mischievously christened the new land 'Greenland', a PR ploy aimed at encouraging further settlement. In fairness to Erik the Fibber, the climate was quite a bit milder when he arrived, but subsequently deteriorated, and by the 15th century the settlers had disappeared (an event much studied by historians). Greenland eventually became a self-governing Danish colony, and today more than 80% of its land is covered in ice.

Iceland was settled by Scandinavians in the 8th and 9th centuries and its 10th-century parliament (the 'Althing') is the oldest in the world. It is one of the most recent large-scale landmasses in the world and was indeed covered in ice during the last ice age, which explains the low numbers of native animal species (the arctic fox is the only native mammal). The two main theories about the origin of the name 'Iceland' are (a) the impressive first sight of its glaciers, (b) a peevish report of a desolate land from a dyspeptic Viking (who seems to have settled later in Iceland). The theory that the name was given in order to discourage immigration is not true. The land was free, not much different from Norway, and the settlers came gladly, often escaping from old feuds and a tired, constricted supply of land.

Dolphins are not as friendly as their smiles suggest

The apparent friendliness of dolphins towards humans has been recorded since the Bronze Age, with several references in ancient Greek art and literature. Even killer whales (actually the largest of the dolphins, and the apex predator of the ocean) do not seem to have ever attacked humans and have learned to cooperate with human fishermen to share fish catches. Yet though the affinity is well attested, much popular thinking about dolphins is rather woolly. Dolphins are often seen as superior beings, both more intelligent and somehow more spiritual than us.

In Robert Merle's novel, *The Day of the Dolphin* (1969), dolphins learn to talk and we find out that they formerly worshipped humans but have now learned to distrust us for all the obvious reasons. We are simply not as nice as they thought we were. Curiously, this is just the conclusion many writers of 'pop science' pieces are increasingly saying about dolphins themselves: they are not that cuddly and the 'friendly' smile is more that of a psycho killer.

It is certainly true that dolphin society is far from being an idealised version of a hippie commune. The most common dolphin 'type', the bottlenose dolphin (familiar to generations of children through the *Flipper* TV series of the 1960s and 1970s), has been closely studied. Bottlenose dolphin groups are often strictly hierarchical. Sometimes male dolphins will form alliances to capture unwilling females for sex. There is strong evidence for what in humans would be called 'infanticide' among dolphins. It has also been known for some time now that dolphins attack and kill harbour porpoises in Scotland's Moray Firth. One suggested explanation for this is that human activity in the Firth was disrupting the dolphin's sonar, causing them to attack their sonar-using relatives, but similarly lethal behaviour has been observed off the Virginia coast, where young dolphins have been killed by adults of their own species.

Dolphins are highly successful animals and have been interacting with humans for millennia, yet it turns out we don't really know them very well at all. It has been suggested that the lone dolphins that seem to enjoy human company so much may be outcasts from their pods who 'make do' by interacting with humans. It has certainly become clear that we need to stop regarding dolphins as either cuddly toys or semi-divine beings (or as food, as in Japan).

Polar bears do not encounter penguins in the wild

In the words of one of Coca-Cola's vice-presidents at Christmas 2005: 'Our special holiday message of *Give. Live. Love. Coke.* reminds people to come together and share the magic of the season and the spirit of generosity, just as our polar bears, penguins and Santa do.' Despite the persistence of advertisers, and the makers of cartoons such as *The Little Polar Bear* (2001), the fact is that polar bears and penguins live at opposite ends of the earth and never meet.

Polar bears are huge carnivores (*see **Polar bears are black***) and would readily make a meal of a penguin (instead they eat small whales, such as beluga), but the distance to get to a penguin is just too big for it to happen. It is a long way from the Arctic to the Galapagos Islands, where the nearest penguins live. Some of the Galapagos penguins (whose total population is pretty small at less than 10,000 and shrinking) can be found on the northern part of the Galapagos Archipelago and are thus the only penguins living in the Northern hemisphere.

The flightless Great Auk, *Pinguïnus impennis,* which used to be distributed from Canada to Scandinavia, would have been hunted over part of its range by polar bears, but humans hunted the species to extinction in the early 19th century.

Other animals suffer from habitat confusion in popular culture. Hollywood has always liked to have its lions living in the African jungle, but of course they are a savanna animal and few wild lions have ever even seen a jungle.

Not in so many words

"All that glitters is not gold." The actual words in one of the false caskets in *The Merchant of Venice* are "All that glisters is not gold; / Often have you heard that told." When Portia bids farewell to the Prince who chose deceiving gold, she says: "A gentle riddance" (not "good riddance", though this phrase *is* used in *Troilus and Cressida*).

God likes beetles

During the course of a lecture in April 1951 the biologist J B S Haldane (who was an atheist) observed that 'the Creator, if He exists, has a special preference for beetles'. He also noted '…and so we might be more likely to meet them than any other type of animal on a planet that would support life'. Beetles are enormously successful on earth: there are around 400,000 species with lots more doubtless waiting to be discovered, and they occupy niches all over, so Haldane's point seems quite sound. There are actually more species of beetles than there are plant species. Beetles are very good at survival and will cope in just about any environment, whereas humans need to exist in a narrow climate band or an artificially maintained approximation of it. The future looks OK for beetles.

Apart from beetles, God also likes bacteria, which seem to occupy every niche available and are even more numerous than beetles. Indeed, some would say that humans are simply bacteria colonies. The bacteria farm us – without their continual operations on us we would die very quickly – and when we do eventually die we provide a lovely delayed feast for them. The future also looks good for bacteria.

Urban foxes may kill your cat

Until quite recently, wildlife experts would confidently say that urban foxes do not attack domestic cats, let alone kill them. Stories of killer urban foxes were, they claimed, nothing more than urban myths. Indeed, cats and foxes were even said to cooperate with each other. One child's natural history book of the 1980s had a charming illustration of a cat on an improbably low bird table swinging a bird feeder in the direction of a waiting fox.

Until a few years ago, British cat owners who claimed their pets had indeed been attacked by foxes were dismissed as misinterpreting the evidence. Wildlife experts would say that a larger cat or perhaps a dog had attacked the cat in question, or if it was a fox it must have been ill. The remains of cats have often been found at fox earths, but this has been explained away as scavenged roadkill.

It's true that in normal circumstances a fox and a cat will recognize each other's presence, but will keep apart from each other, maintaining the kind of studied indifference common where evenly matched predators represent no real threat to each other. But the brutal truth is that, as with all predation, the kill comes down to size, opportunity and hunger. Foxes will certainly take kittens if they get the chance, and cats will kill undefended cubs. If the fox is very hungry it will even try to take a small adult cat. A leading factor in the increase in such incidents in British cities is allegedly the replacement of old-fashioned household bins with larger communal 'wheelie bins'. Foxes can easily overturn the former, but can't get into the latter – in other words, a major food source has been blocked off. Pest controllers in various cities have reported increased attacks on cats by foxes following the spread of wheelie bins.

Other issues tend to muddy the issue, unfortunately: campaigners against field sports assume that stories about cat-killing foxes somehow harm the case against foxhunting, and people who support foxhunting have a vested interest in portraying foxes as bloodthirsty killers who must be kept in check. Neither view, however, has any relevance to the question of the extent and nature of urban fox predation on domestic cats, which certainly seems to be on the increase.

There are no killer dolphins in the Gulf of Mexico

On 25 September 2005, *The Observer* printed what it called 'the oddest tale to emerge from the aftermath of Hurricane Katrina. Armed dolphins, trained by the US military to shoot terrorists and pinpoint spies underwater, may be missing in the Gulf of Mexico'. It went on to say that 'experts' believed that the dolphins (36 in number), which had escaped from a marine compound, may 'shoot at divers in wetsuits', as that is what they have been trained to do.

The report is nonsense. The story that some dolphins were washed out to sea in the wake of Hurricane Katrina does indeed appear to be true. Eight dolphins belonging to the Marine Life Aquarium were washed out to sea and were later recovered. But there were no 'killer dolphins' on the loose. The US Navy does use dolphins for mine detection and locating lost swimmers. It is of course just possible that the US Navy is keeping quiet about more aggressive training programmes, but as sceptics point out, training dolphins to pick out America's enemies and destroy them while not launching missiles at allies, seems madly implausible.

It seems *The Observer* relied upon one source for its 'killer dolphin' story. This source had previously told the paper in 1998 that 22 dolphins washed ashore in the French Mediterranean had been killed by the US Navy. The same source was apparently responsible for stories about crop circles (*The Observer*) and the alleged true cause of Amy Johnson's death (*The Guardian*). This is not to question the reliability of the source, simply that some reflection may be required before any newspaper prints more scary stories about killer dolphins.

Snakes are not charmed by music

The image of a snake charmer playing his instrument to bring a snake (usually a cobra) out of its basket, swaying in time to the music, is one of the iconic visions of the mystic east (*see also* **No one has ever been seen to disappear up an Indian rope**), or more usually these days, North Africa. The picture also harks back to an even older European myth: the calming effect Orpheus had on the animals with his music. 'Charming' snakes with music is a pleasing reflection of the power of human art over the natural world. Except that it's bunkum. Snakes are deaf to airborne sounds and cannot hear a note of the 'charming' music. What makes them sway is the motion of the charmer's pipe.

A popular place to see snake charming is in Morocco and other parts of North Africa, where such spectacles are lucrative performances. In fact, these spectacles are not aimed at tourists in the first instance: they are for local consumption and are designed to sell magic spells and charms that will protect the purchaser from snakes and other evils. Tourists in places such as Marrakech who are cajoled into having their photographs taken with the snakes, are unwittingly helping to perpetuate a peculiarly horrible tradition.

The snake species typically involved (cobras, vipers and puff adders) certainly look the part, but are completely harmless. They have had their lips sewn up, leaving only a small space for the tongue to project through. The snakes die of hunger and infection and are then replaced with fresh snakes. (Snake charmers in India, however, where there is a long Hindu tradition of venerating snakes, often treat their snakes well.)

The parallel idea that snakes themselves 'charm' their prey, particularly birds, by hypnotizing them – with unblinking stares and mesmeric swaying – is also a popular notion, but there is no truth in it either. If a snake takes a bird on a nest it is because the bird is sleeping or is defending its young.

Bats are the most successful mammal

Candidates for the 'most successful' mammal include humans (these creatures manage to inhabit and exploit a huge variety of environments) and human hangers-on, such as cats, dogs and, since the creation of large human habitation sites, rats and mice. In fact, bats are the most successful mammal. Estimates of bat numbers vary, but they are huge: only rats come anywhere near in terms of overall numbers. In the tropics there are very likely more bats than all other mammals combined. Enormous colonies have been found, and the bat population of a single site, Deer Cave in Borneo, is estimated to exceed three million. And in terms of species, there are almost 1,000 species of bat. There is a total of around 4,450 species of mammals, so this makes bats the most prolific species of mammal.

Bats are odd creatures, and the subject of numerous misconceptions. They look like winged rodents and many people assume they are related to mice. In fact, they may have a close relationship with primates and, despite appearances, are more closely related to humans than to rodents. A popular superstition is that bats are dirty; in fact, they are very clean. The most bizarre misconception about bats – that they are likely to get tangled in your hair – is of course also nonsense. Bats are very good at finding their way about and are extremely unlikely to hit your head, either by accident or on purpose.

The smallest mammal in the world is a bat from Thailand, Kitti's Hog-nosed Bat, which is just over an inch long and weighs 0.07 oz. The scariest mammal in the human imagination is perhaps the vampire bat, but the only threat to humans from a vampire bat is the (admittedly alarming) possibility that the bat is a rabies carrier. In fact, a bee sting is statistically more likely to give you problems than a vampire bat bite. About 70% of bats are insectivorous, with most of the rest feeding on flowers and fruits. Apart from vampire bats, there are only a very few carnivorous bats, including Australia's ghost bat, which will hunt anything it can carry, including other bats.

Bulls do not get infuriated at the sight of red

The idea that bulls get mad at the sight of a red cloak or flag being waved at them stems of course from Spanish bullfights. This has led to much low humour from *The Beano* downwards, with a typical human protagonist wearing something red as he marches across a field, thus driving a previously unseen bull into such a state of frenzy that it charges the unfortunate human, who has to leap over a hedge for safety. A favourite detail in such cartoons is a red patch on the trousers so the bull can toss the patch-wearer out of the field.

In fact, bulls aren't at all bothered about the colour red, as, like most cattle, they are colour-blind. In a bullfight, it is the movement of the matador's red cloak that attracts them (*see Snakes are not charmed by music*) and if they are in a foul mood it is because they are in pain from the barbed darts (*banderillas*) embedded in their flanks.

The bull myth was included in a list of fallacies by George Orwell in his *Tribune* column in 1944, after being told by a barmaid that dipping your moustache in beer turns it flat. 'Only later did it strike me that this was probably one of those superstitions which are able to keep alive because they have the air of being scientific truths.' The fallacies listed by Orwell are the red-enraged bull one; a swan can break your leg with a blow of its wing; if you cut yourself between the thumb and forefinger you'll get lockjaw; washing your hands in the water eggs have been boiled in gives you warts; sulphur in a dog's drinking water acts as a tonic; and powdered glass will kill you (*see Powdered glass is not poisonous*).

As Orwell's list shows, some popular myths and fallacies fade as culture and behaviour changes (few men these days have moustaches to dip accidentally into their pints of beer), while other myths seem indestructible, like the one about the power of the swan's wing.

You may share more DNA with a chimp than an African elephant does with an Asian elephant

Terms such as genetic 'code' and 'genome' and even the much more common term 'DNA' are flung about with such abandon in the popular press that any surprising claims you read should be carefully examined. Yet some of the more startling claims are actually true. The ponderously named Chimpanzee Sequencing and Analysis Consortium has analysed the genetic code of chimpanzees and concluded that chimps and humans share almost 99% of the most significant areas of DNA. Humans and chimps derive from a mutual ancestor, and the separation between us dates from about 6 million years ago. However distant this might seem, chimps are indeed our closest living relatives.

Although to our eyes there seems to be no great difference between African and Asian elephants (apart from size) and horses and zebras (apart from stripes – *see also* **Mr Ed was not a zebra**), genetic research is throwing up some remarkable conclusions. It was discovered in 2001 that there are actually three species of elephant: the Asian and now two African ones, the savanna version and the forest elephant. Astonishingly, the forest and savanna species are further apart from each other genetically than tigers are from lions, or horses from zebras.

Tragically, we are only discovering how close we are to chimps just at the point in time where we are driving chimpanzees and the other great apes ever closer to extinction, whether through habitat destruction in southeast Asia or the bushmeat trade in Africa.

Not in so many words

"Because it's there." This remark was reported in *The New York Times* in 1923 as mountaineer George Mallory's response to the question "why climb Everest?" Whether he used these exact words has been doubted, but Edmund Hillary's more down-to-earth comment on climbing the mountain in 1953 is well attested: "Well, we knocked the bastard off!"

The British love of whales is a recent phenomenon

The appearance of a whale in the River Thames in January 2006 caused great excitement in the British media, an excitement that – as with the death of Princess Diana – became one of those rare media feeding frenzies that genuinely replicated the feelings of the population at large. People tuned in in their millions to 24-hour news channels to watch live footage of the whale in the water, while TV commentators observed that whales were traditionally of great importance to the British people.

It all seemed a quite normal response, and the emotional involvement of the British people was clear, yet in fact it was a very untraditional response to a whale in trouble. The last time a whale had been so far up the Thames was in 1961, when a 16ft minke whale got as far as Kew Bridge. Along the way it capsized a dinghy and a man was drowned. The police in boats escorted the beast about until it died. To the public at large, the whale was a curiosity, no more. There were no floods of tears as the carcass was towed away, and small boys stationed along the river regretfully put the stones back in their pockets.

The 1961 indifference is quite striking. Virginia Woolf said there was a change in human character in 1910, a date she says is both symbolic and arbitrary, but which reflects something that did happen to human nature. Something similar seems to have happened in Britain in the 1960s, and whales and their songs have became something to love.

The response of past centuries to a whale in the water would undoubtedly have been to kill the whale – for profit. London used to be a major consumer of whale oil, and it was what kept the London streets lit at night before gas lighting was introduced in the early 19th century.

Farmers do not always know best about country matters

It is a commonplace that only country folk have a proper understanding of rural matters. More generally, it has often been assumed that farmers must have great knowledge of the wildlife and landscape that surrounds them. Yet the idea that farmers are necessarily caring custodians of the landscape and its wildlife does not bear too close an examination, despite what we might learn from *The Archers*. Farmers are not noticeably interested in the country's heritage, any more than any other profession. A Scottish farmer once upended and broke a standing stone that had in all likelihood been in position for more than 2,000 years. Remonstrated with, he replied 'it's just a stane'. From his point of view, he had a living to make and the 'stane' got in the way.

Farming ignorance of the animals they share their lands with goes way back, perhaps further back than the upended standing stone. There can be few 'townies' who have held bizarre beliefs capable of matching those of farmers about wildlife, as the history of the humble hedgehog shows. Up until modern times farmers would routinely kill hedgehogs as they believed that they sucked milk from cows. Dogs were trained specifically for the task of hunting and killing hedgehogs, animals which are actually of value to farmers as they eat pests such as slugs.

The poet John Clare believed with others that hedgehogs, in a lovely image, collected crab apples on their spines and stored them underground, but even he knew that the milk theft story was just a myth: in his poem on the hedgehog, he contrasts the gypsies' hunt for hedgehogs to eat with the farmers' ignorant killing of the innocent beasts:

> But still they hunt the hedges all about
> And shepherd dogs are trained to hunt them out
> They hurl with savage force the stick and stone
> And no one cares and still the strife goes on.

Amateur 19th-century naturalists such as Clare knew far more about the wild animals on farmland than the farmers did. Eventually, in a slow process, naturalists have gradually educated British farmers into recognizing the merits of wild animals, and the folly of the indiscriminate killing of anything with teeth and claws, yet even golden eagles and other rare birds of prey are still being killed by farmers and by gamekeepers on 'sporting' estates. In America, farmers will kill as a matter of course any non-venomous snakes they find on their property, although garter snakes, for example, are far more efficient rodent controllers than cats (and they also drive away rattlesnakes).

➤ *See also* **Cheese is bad for mice and milk is bad for hedgehogs.**

Food and Drink

Beer is better than water

Water is a pretty dangerous substance. It's a very good home for bacteria, and although we clearly need it to live, we ought to be very careful with it. Even in normally safe Britain, many hillwalkers will have had the experience of gulping cool fresh running water, then finding a dead and maggoty sheep further upstream.

We are all familiar with cartoons of men crawling out of the desert towards a waterhole, but the likely outcome of drinking oasis water will be severe stomach cramps at best. On the other hand, alcohol is very good at countering water-borne pathogens (not only is it toxic to them, but the boiling process when using malt kills pathogens), and beer contains nutrients (pure water shouldn't contain any!).

Unfortunately, alcohol is also very good at dehydrating the body, so drinks that include it make you want to drink more, which will then make you even thirstier. This problem was encountered and solved in ancient times by producing beer with a very low alcohol content, thus creating a safe method of consuming water, and a transportable one too (the first carry-outs were for health reasons). There is evidence on Sumerian clay tablets from around 4000 BC that the Sumerians used beer for all sorts for purposes, from religion to medicine (and innkeepers who overcharged could be drowned). The Babylonians had at least 16 different kinds of beer, and their *Codex Hammurabi*, one of the earliest written compilations of human laws, dating from c. 1850 BC, includes regulations for preparing and distributing beer.

This very low alcohol form of beer is familiar to us from the world of Elizabethan plays, where the drinking of 'small beer' is commonplace. Women seem to have been central to the production and serving of beer. From Babylon to modern times, and from the fictional worlds of Mistress Quickly to Bet Lynch, the beer industry has seen women in key roles, though not in the Middle Ages, when abbeys dominated the trade. The European abbeys, which often produced beers to varying strengths for sale, began to lose their power when

24

the German Emperor Sigismund cancelled the abbeys' tax-free status around 1400, freeing the way for taxable commercial breweries to flourish: beer, it seems, has always been big business.

Carrots have no vitamin A

If you search for advice on nutrition, you will often find instructions to eat carrots because they are rich in vitamin A. However, other sources will assure you there is no vitamin A in carrots.

In fact, carrots have no vitamin A, but they are very rich in betacarotene, which can (but not invariably) convert into vitamin A in your body. Eating too many carrots can indeed turn your skin orange, or at least a tad yellowish. An excess of vitamin A in the body can be toxic, making you feel tired and perhaps nauseous, but it is probably impossible to overdose on carrots and make yourself seriously ill: the body seems capable of taking what it needs from the betacarotene to make vitamin A.

Carrots have an anti-fungus compound called falcarinol which may also be protective against cancer, and eating carrots is indeed good for your eyesight. Vitamin A helps maintain the eye's surface linings and keeps harmful bacteria out.

An EU jam directive of 1979 allegedly considers carrots to be fruit, as carrot marmalade has long been popular in Portugal, but this particular directive seems to have been worded in order to get some consistency into legal requirements for fruit (or, if Portuguese, carrot) content in jam, so seems to be a perfectly sensible piece of legislation rather than an example of the EU looniness so beloved by the British press.

If you want to go into carrots and their wonders in a big way there is an online World Carrot Museum full of useful carrot information (including reproductions of Old Master paintings of carrots).

Cheese is bad for mice and milk is bad for hedgehogs

Providing food for pets (or companion, or captive animals) is a process that is easy to get wrong, as indeed is supplying food to wild animals. A still very common myth (propagated on some advice-offering websites, alas) has it that mice (and other rodents such as rats) have a particular liking for cheese. Cheese is actually very bad for mice and rats. It has traditionally been used to bait mousetraps because it smells, and has the right texture for impaling on the trap. Mice and rats are omnivores and their owners need to take expert advice on what to feed them. Rats are on the whole more delicate feeders than mice, and more conservative in their diet, but both types of rodents are, when kept by the ill-informed, more likely to get cheddar than oatmeal.

Unlike rodents, hedgehogs are carnivores and eat a wide range of prey, mostly invertebrates such as beetles and earthworms. A dish of milk, especially topped up with slices of bread, is wholly inappropriate food for them. Hedgehog numbers have been declining sharply in the UK since the beginning of the 21st century, and while it is unlikely that saucers of milk are the main reason, they certainly don't help. Most animals are lactose intolerant to cow's milk (cows excepted, of course), and a regular supply of milk and bread will pile on layers of killer fat.

Notices at zoos telling people not to feed the animals are frequently ignored, as all zookeepers will confirm. Dolphins can have cheeseburgers thrown at them, and polar bears have been known to get Penguins (the biscuit, that is). Readers of this book will know just how ill-informed this particular joke is (*see **Polar bears do not encounter penguins in the wild***).

Captivity is not natural and the food supply for animals must be organized to take that into account. The most common form of death for captive animals is likely to be overfeeding, followed by incorrect feeding. It is not helpful, for example, to feed live mice and rats to snakes (and is anyway illegal in the UK). Snakes would not cope well in captivity with the parasites they would get from live prey; frozen rodents have dead parasites and are healthier for the snake.

➤ *See also **Farmers do not always know best about country matters**.*

Coca-Cola did not invent the red Santa and never contained much cocaine

There are many tales in circulation about Coca-Cola, and some of them are even true. But one of the most common – that Coca-Cola invented Santa's red costume and before that it was always green is not true (oddly, there are stories that the original Coke was actually green coloured). Coca-Cola was invented in the late 19th century, and Coca-Cola's first jolly Santa (created by the artist Haddon Sundblom) only appeared as recently as 1931, four years after *The New York Times* described the standard Santa as having a hood, white whiskers and 'red garments'.

Red Santas go way back before the invention of Coca-Cola's. It has been claimed that there is an identifiable 'Father Christmas' figure with a red cloak in a (presumably hand-coloured) 17th-century woodcut, but there are lots of verifiable examples of mid 19th-century Santas in red (and indeed green and other colours). The 'standard' Santa developed slowly: an artist called Thomas Nast in *Harper's Weekly* gave us Santas in various sizes (from elf-like to barrel-shaped) but with the fur and whiskers we have come to expect. In the late 1880s a Boston printer called Louis Prang drew red-clad Santas for Christmas cards and our modern Santa took his final rotund shape.

Another common myth about Coke is that it originally contained cocaine. Coca-Cola was originally marketed as a patent medicine that would cure, among other ailments, impotence and addiction to morphine. The drink contained coca leaves, and at first quite a large amount of them; but pure cocaine is a very expensive extract from coca leaves, far too expensive for a five-cent glass of fizz. There would certainly have been traces of cocaine from the leaves in the drink, but no one drank coke to get a cocaine high. Indeed, it would have been physically impossible to consume the required amount of liquid.

Coca-Cola has, of course, become a worldwide symbol of American corporate dominance and as such is open to attack on all fronts, from battling rival drinks such as Mecca-Cola to facing accusations of human rights abuses in India and Colombia as a result of the company's employment policies. The company's relationship with the Hitler regime has been much debated. One of Coca-Cola's most popular products, Fanta, was in fact invented by a resourceful employee in wartime Nazi Germany as a Coke substitute.

Coffee does not sober you up

You've seen it often enough in old westerns. The drunken doctor (Thomas Mitchell in *Stagecoach* is the archetype) is faced with a woman giving birth (preferably with marauding 'Injuns' banging at the door) and calls for hot water and coffee – to sober up he drinks the coffee in gallons. What he does with the hot water is not revealed, but it is certain that the coffee won't be doing him much good (what he actually needs to do is drink lots of water).

After consuming alcohol, you need time to regain sobriety. Coffee will do you no good, neither will a cold shower, not even (despite its use in various Westerns) under a hand-operated well pump. If you are an average individual, alcohol needs to depart your system at a regular rate of approximately 0.015% of blood alcohol content per hour. (This is called the BAC number.) If you have 10 times 0.015% you have a BAC of .15% and you will need 10 hours before you are completely sober and fit to deliver babies. This holds true whether you are male, female, fit or unfit, or weigh 10 or 20 stone.

Coffee is said to have the effect of speeding up the alcohol rushing round your system and therefore sobering you up quicker, but all you are actually doing is adding another toxin to your system: no one seems to know all the bad effects there might be from hitting your body with a large dose of coffee on top of a large dose of alcohol; there will certainly be no benefits and most certainly a lot of drawbacks.

The problems associated with alcohol have been known for millennia, the problems associated with coffee are perhaps less well known. Caffeine is one of the most widely used drugs on the planet, is habit-forming, and induces states of tension, the psychological and physiological effects are many and complex. The health implications of consuming large amounts of coffee are pretty severe: it may even, in sufficiently large overdoses, stimulate psychosis, though a potentially lethal dose of caffeine would require the consumption of something like 150 cups or more.

Not in so many words

"Come up and see me sometime." The words Mae West actually drawls in *She Done Him Wrong* (1933) are: "Why don't you come up sometime, see me?"

Haggis is not originally or solely Scottish

'Get yer haggis, right here. Chopped heart 'n' lungs. Boiled in a wee sheep's stomach. Tastes as good as it sounds. Good for what ails ye!' Thus speaks Groundskeeper Willie in an episode of *The Simpsons*, vainly trying to sell haggis to the people of Springfield who, like everyone else, identify this dish as Scottish.

Willie's description is incomplete: the classic haggis comprises heart, lungs and liver (any of which can derive from either sheep or calf), chopped up with suet, onions and oatmeal, all sewn up in the 'wee sheep's stomach' and boiled (remembering to leave a bit of slack to avoid a disastrous explosion during cooking).

The word itself is Middle English, and *Chambers Dictionary* says it possibly derives from the Anglo-French word 'hageis', from 'haguer', to cut up. Other plausible derivations are from the Swedish 'hagga' (to chop) or from the Old French 'agace' for magpie, the latter being based on the supposition that the wide-ranging collecting habits of the magpie are comparable to the varied contents of a haggis (the unwary should be reminded at this point that the very subject of haggis attracts jokes, wild speculation and wind-ups).

Haggis is not specifically Scottish, however. People have been making something like it for at least 2,000 years. Certainly the Romans had something very similar if not identical. It is basically a way of making offal palatable and eking out the remains of an animal, and thus occurs in many shepherding cultures. The Scottish connection with haggis has become established worldwide for cultural reasons, partly because of Burns Suppers, partly because many people suppose that Scottish food is offal-based (and not just awful).

Willie's haggis will have been homemade, as the United States Department of Agriculture has determined that sheep lungs are unfit for human consumption – the import of 'authentic' haggis is therefore illegal in the US (several Scottish firms do excellent vegetarian haggises which are certainly native to Scotland and perfectly exportable to the US).

There is one influential American unlikely to be lobbying for a revision to the ban on imported haggis. At the G8 summit held at Gleneagles in July 2005, George W Bush had this to say on haggis:

INTERVIEWER: And I wondered if you had any plans for a celebration, that may or may not include haggis?

PRESIDENT BUSH: Yes, haggis. I was briefed on haggis. No. (*Laughter*) Generally, on your birthday you – my mother used to say, 'What do you want to eat?' and I don't ever remember saying 'Haggis, Mom'.

The Middle Eastern taboo on eating pigs has nothing to do with worms

Two of the monotheist religions with their origins in the Middle East, Judaism and Islam, prohibit their adherents from eating pork. A third, Christianity, has no problem at all with pork consumption. It is commonly said that the prohibition makes sense in the Middle East as pigs in hot countries are infested with intestinal parasites that will be passed on to humans when consumed and make them ill. The prohibition is seen as an ancient adaptive health measure and makes perfect sense.

The parasite argument seems plausible but is unlikely to be true. Other peoples in hot countries happily eat pork without having developed any such taboo. A darker reason for the prohibition may be that soft ground is not too common in the Middle East and bodies have traditionally not been buried very deep. Pigs are omnivores and gladly scavenge dead meat such as human corpses. The rather convincing argument here is that it is hard to tuck into something that has just eaten your granny and will eat you when your turn comes.

Many cultures also have taboos on eating dogs. Dogs have been used as hunting companions for humans for hundreds of thousands of years, but that wouldn't in itself have been enough to save them from being eaten (horses are also used by humans but are eaten in practically all cultures except English-speaking ones). What has saved dogs in many cultures is that they, like pigs, are sanitary devices, and have traditionally been used to clean up human habitation by eating what humans leave. This may also include human bodies, unfortunately. Some cultures have a relish for puppy meat, and it seems it is OK to eat dog before it gets a chance to eat your relatives.

Goats performed a similar scavenging role in some Norwegian mountain areas, and where they performed this function, were not eaten by humans. As always, however, human culture is remarkably diverse, and it has also been suggested that the Jews acquired the reluctance to eat pigs from the Egyptians, the pig being a cult animal of the god Seth.

Powdered glass is not poisonous

George Orwell's list of fallacies (*see **Bulls do not get infuriated at the sight of red***) includes the widespread notion that finely powdered glass is an effective poison: 'it is so widespread that in India, for instance, people are constantly trying to poison one another with powdered glass, with disappointing results'. That powdered glass is an effective method of murder is still widely believed and will occasionally turn up in crime novels and TV dramas.

It all comes down to a question of quantity. There have never been any recognized benefits of ingesting powdered glass, so no one would take it willingly. Yet the proposed victim could only have a very small amount introduced into his or her food without it becoming noticeable. Large bits of glass would certainly cause problems if taken internally but would be detected soon enough in one's risotto.

The fallacy of 'poisonous' powdered glass was long ago exposed by Sir Thomas Browne in his *Pseudodoxia Epidemica, or Vulgar Errors* (1646): 'That Glass is poison, according unto common conceit, I know not how to grant. Not onely from the innocency of its ingredients, that is, fine Sand, and the ashes of Glass-wort or Fearn, which in themselves are harmless and useful; ... but also from experience, as having given unto Dogs above a dram thereof, subtilly powdered in Butter and Paste, without any visible disturbance.'

Sandwiches were invented for work

As is well known, John Montagu, 4th Earl of Sandwich (1718-1792), invented the sandwich. The story goes that Sandwich was gambling (as usual) and did not want to leave the game to eat, so he told his long-suffering butler to make something he could eat at the card table. The butler placed a slice of meat between two pieces of bread, the wheeze was copied by the other gamers, who were soon all sitting round the gambling table holding their meals in one hand, and thus the 'sandwich' was born. The story sounds plausible, but one wonders about the state of the cards and the gaming table felt after a few hours of aristocratic grease being dripped onto them... In fact, the tale was probably put in circulation to underline the Earl's reputation for dissipation.

The sandwich was much more likely to have been invented as a workplace snack, to give the Earl more time at his desk, rather than at the gambling table. While not, perhaps, the most likeable of men, he was in fact largely respected for his hard work and industry, if not his brains. He was certainly a very busy man, becoming Secretary of State and Postmaster General, but his best-known post was as First Lord of the Admiralty 1748-51, 1763, and finally during that very busy period when the Americans revolted, 1771-82 (some claim his incompetence hastened the American victory).

In 1778, Captain Cook 'discovered' and dutifully named the Sandwich Islands after the Earl (who was effectively his boss) but the archipelago was long ago renamed as Hawaii. The South Sandwich Islands in the South Atlantic still serve as a memorial to the Earl's activities away from the card table.

Spices were not used to disguise the taste of rotten meat in the Middle Ages

The notion that spices were used to mask the odour and taste of meat that had gone off used to be something of an orthodoxy in teaching about the Middle Ages, perhaps because it fitted in with a general notion of medieval Europeans being dirty and ill-educated. The fable persists in the media, and also in recipe books, but is complete nonsense.

Spices were very expensive in medieval Europe and there is no record anywhere of anyone being stupid enough to use them to disguise the flavour of bad meat. If you had enough money to buy spices, you certainly had enough money to buy good meat. The so-called 'Age of Exploration' of the 15th to 17th centuries was originally driven by the spice trade, a trade that goes way back. Pepper, for example, which has always been one of the main spices, was sourced by the Romans from India.

People have added spices to food since the invention of the skewer and the cooking pot, but the medicinal value of spices, such as the antiseptic property of cloves, has also long been recognized. Cloves (from the Spice Islands) have been used in China for around 2,000 years, but became increasingly sought after in Europe in the early Middle Ages, and the wealth from the trade helped make Venice a major power. Magellan's circumnavigation of the globe (1519-22) was a costly enterprise (four of his five ships were lost) but the single remaining ship returned with enough cloves and nutmeg to make the trip a financial success (though not for Magellan himself, who had been killed in the Phillipines).

Spinach will not make you strong

Spinach is a plant of the goosefoot family, and its leaves are well-known as food. The plant originated in Asia, then came to Europe through Persia around the 15th century, so we have been eating it for longer than potatoes or tomatoes, which came from the Americas. The supposed health-giving properties of spinach were established early in the 20th century. In World War I, wounded French soldiers were given wine fortified with spinach in order to help them recover by filling them with iron so they could go back to the Front (no doubt they were suitably grateful…).

The idea that spinach has a high iron content is in fact based on a transcription error. In 1870 a Dr von Wolf put a decimal point in the wrong place and it became a 'scientific fact' (until the error was spotted in 1937) that spinach contained ten times more iron than it actually does. In fact, even the iron it does contain is of no use to us as spinach actually 'steals' iron from our body by encouraging its excretion. The iron in spinach is bound up with oxalic acid that seems to inhibit its absorption into your bloodstream, as do phytates

(phytates can be countered with citrus fruit, so stick a slice or two of orange on your spinach salad). Popeye would probably have done better hitting Bluto with cans of spinach rather than eating the stuff inside (NB: a common misconception about Popeye is that he has big biceps: not true. Once spinached, he has very large forearm muscles; his biceps are actually quite modest).

Spinach does, however, contain antioxidants and vitamins A, C and K and other goodies. A nice spinach and potato curry (with a glass of orange juice) will very probably do you the world of good.

Strawberries are false fruit, but tomatoes may be real fruit

As the UK government reminds us in its beguilingly entitled document, *Tomatoes are not the only fruit – a guide to controlled vocabularies*, the scientific principle of 'polyhierarchical taxonomy' means that in a taxonomic chart 'tomatoes' can be classed under 'fruit' by those who think like botanists, or under 'vegetables' by the rest of us. In a traditional taxonomy, each item exists only once, and in one place. Thus 'tomato' will be botanically classified under 'vine fruit', which is in turn under 'fruit'. In a 'polyhierarchical' system, on the other hand (or branch), tomatoes are in their traditional botanic taxonomic structure, but are also linked to vegetables in a parallel structure – so in this taxonomy, tomatoes are linked with carrots in that both are 'salad' vegetables (and carrots, in their turn, can also be 'root' vegetables). A 'controlled vocabulary', such as this means that the government can speak of things in the same terms as the rest of us (or at least part of the time).

Jeanette Winterson told us that *Oranges are not the Only Fruit* (1985), as indeed they are not, but some fruits are not quite fruit. The strawberry, for example, is not a 'true' fruit, but a 'false' one. It is the base of the flower, and not a growth from the flower's ovary: hence it is not a true berry. All very botanically pedantic – the most meaningful difference is within strawberries, of course: between savouring the taste of a wild strawberry, small, but intensely flavoured, and the completely different experience of eating its sad, forced, pesticided store-bought cousin.

Much else that we eat is not quite what it seems. Peanuts, for example, are not nuts but legumes. Legumes have seed pods that split along the sides when ripe. So, strictly, peanuts belong with lentils and peas rather than with Brazil nuts.

> ### Not in so many words
> "Come with me to the Casbah." This line is often said to come from the film *Algiers* (1938) but does not. In fact, the Charles Boyer character, Pepe le Moko, can never *leave* the Casbah, which is both his refuge from the police, and a virtual prison. (The animator Chuck Jones based the love-struck skunk Pepe le Pew on Boyer's Pepe le Moko).

Vegetarians do not have lower iron levels

It is commonly supposed that vegetarians must have low iron levels because they do not eat meat. Why a meat-free diet should be held to be iron-deficient is rarely made explicit: it seems to be a general assumption that the consumption of animal flesh is necessary to keep your iron levels up to a healthy level. Doctors have been known to tell vegetarians that they are likely to have a low iron level and should not give blood – especially if they are female. But as every vegetarian platelet or whole blood donor knows, vegetarians and indeed vegans are very welcome at blood donor centres: they tend to watch what they eat, are generally healthy and will not have nasty stuff from intensively reared meat lurking in their system. And their iron levels will not necessarily be lower than those of omnivore blood donors.

A well-known study of iron levels among vegetarians is that of Draper & Wheeler (1989), a study of vegetarians in London that found no indication at all of iron deficiency. The evidence from epidemiological studies seems fairly clear: all other factors being equal, vegetarians live longer than omnivores, and have no deficiencies in the level of anything at all in their blood.

Music and Musicians

Albinoni did not write his Adagio

Albinoni's Adagio is perhaps classical music's most noted affirmation of Noel Coward's remark (in *Private Lives*) about the potency of cheap music. Like Barber's Adagio, it has become a multipurpose 'sad' piece of music to be played over images of war, death, heartbreak, etc. Repetition dulls the effect but, like the Barber piece, the Adagio is fine music. We've all just heard it a bit too often.

Tomaso Albinoni (1671-1751) was a Venetian composer, much of whose surviving work is now popular. But not a lot has survived. The bulk of his manuscript compositions were held in the Dresden State Library, and were destroyed in the firebombing of the city by Allied aircraft at the end of WWII. The truth is that Albinoni never heard his famous Adagio and would very likely not have recognized it if he did. The piece of music we now have is a reconstruction by Albinoni's biographer, the Italian scholar Remo Giazotto, who visited Dresden in 1945 to see what he could salvage. Giazotto found a manuscript fragment of a movement from which only the bass line and a few bars of melody survived.

The Adagio is now Albinoni's most famous work, though many argue it should really be called 'Giazotto's Adagio'. Certainly there are lots of compositions in the classical repertoire where the composer still gets the full credit even while including many more 'borrowed' elements than Giazotto took from Albinoni.

Mozart was not buried in a pauper's grave

Despite having been one of the most popular composers of his day, patronized by the nobility, a household name and loved by everyone, poor Mozart was forgotten when, in 1791, he died aged only 35 and was flung into a 'pauper's grave' – or so the story goes. Mozart has remained very popular, and this myth sticks because it fits in with a general conception of the Romantic artist, spurned and neglected by an indifferent society.

In fact, while not terribly fashionable when he died, Mozart was highly regarded by many music lovers and was far from lacking in commissions. He was also still a court musician. The myth of his penury was not helped by his habit of writing frequent begging letters, but he was a spendthrift, rather than poverty-stricken. His income was far above that of the great majority of musicians of his day. The 'pauper's grave' is a complete myth. Mozart was buried in a communal grave (like other members of the 'middling' classes), as required by laws decreed in 1784 as a health measure. The exact location has been lost in the course of time.

Myths abound about Mozart. The story of the deadly rivalry between Mozart and the composer Salieri, which has the latter poisoning Mozart out of jealousy, did emerge in Salieri's lifetime, but no Mozart authority gives any credence to the tale. The myth was given artistic expression by Pushkin in his play *Mozart and Salieri* (1830), and was taken up by Peter Shaffer in his play *Amadeus* (1979), and the subsequent film of Shaffer's play established this as fact in many people's minds. There is actually no evidence of any serious rivalry at all between the two composers.

One very implausible Mozart story is that while on a trip to Rome as a boy, he attended a performance of Allegri's *Miserere* at the Vatican, but could not buy a copy of the score. The Pope, it is said, loved the piece so much he wanted it sung at the Vatican and nowhere else, and the score's publication was therefore banned, but Mozart memorized it and wrote it down. This unlikely tale seems to be substantially true, though we may remain sceptical about some of the attendant details – it is often added, for example, that he revised his first transcription of the score at a second performance, the first version being taken into the performance concealed inside his hat.

You do not have to give up a week of your life to see Wagner's *Ring Cycle*

Richard Wagner's four-opera cycle *The Ring of the Nibelung* was composed over 26 years, from 1848 to 1874, and comprises *The Rhinegold, The Valkyrie, Siegfried* and *The Twilight of the Gods*. Wagner's vision was immense and highly influential. Since the late 19th century, the Ring Cycle has continued to echo (as it were) around western culture, from *Apocalypse Now* to the novels of J R R Tolkien.

It takes roughly 15 hours to listen to a recording of the entire Ring cycle, and that's if you jump straight from one CD to the next. To see the whole cycle in one go – with scene changes and transitions between operas – takes a good bit longer. Remembering Rossini's waspish observation: 'Wagner has lovely moments but awful quarters of an hour', it's easy to see why many people fear the thought of actually settling down to experience this highpoint of 19th century opera.

But fear not: you can see and listen to a boiled-down version that extracts the goodness from the Ring and also throws in the overtures from *The Flying Dutchman* and *Tannhäuser* for good measure. It is, of course, *What's Opera, Doc?* (1957), which, at under 7 minutes, is the greatest value operatic experience of all time. Indeed it was recognized as such by the US Library of Congress on being inducted into the National Film Registry in 1992, which makes it 'among the most culturally, historically or aesthetically significant films of our time'.

The characters in the film are Elmer Fudd and Bugs Bunny. Fudd, as is usual in Warner (as opposed to Wagner) cartoons, pursues Bugs as Siegfried, singing 'kill the wabbit', to the 'Ride of the Valkyries'. Bugs disguises himself as Brunhilde, and Elmer falls in love (sung to a sumptuous orchestral backing) –

> Elmer: Oh, Bwunehiwda, you're so wuvwee.
> Bugs: Yes I know it, I can't help it.

Their dance together was modelled on two classically trained dancers (who had previously modelled for Disney's *Fantasia*). Bugs's helmet falls off, Elmer/Siegfried realizes he has been duped and kills 'the wabbit'. Full of remorse, he carries Bugs tragically off to Valhalla, and the cartoon ends with Bugs saying to camera: 'What did you expect in an opera? A happy ending?'

Beautiful to look at, beautifully acted and sung, *What's Opera, Doc?* is a fine piece of cartoon art and for many will be just the right serving-size of Wagnerian opera.

Elgar was not upset by A C Benson's patriotic setting of 'Land of Hope and Glory'

Sir Edward Elgar wrote the rousing 'Pomp and Circumstance' marches in March 1901. The poet A C Benson suggested he should write some lyrics to the trio section and Elgar thought this a good idea. The setting, which became known as 'Land of Hope and Glory', was subsequently issued as a revised separate piece, and the version first performed in Sheffield in 1902 by the great contralto Clara Butt is the one we know today:

> Land of Hope and Glory,
> Mother of the Free,
> How shall we extol thee,
> Who are born of thee?
> Wider still and wider
> Shall thy bounds be set;
> God, who made thee mighty,
> Make thee mightier yet.

The song has never been universally loved: in fact many people deeply dislike it, and some claim further that Elgar himself loathed it, and indeed stormed out of its premiere, so shocked was he by the absurdly jingoistic patriotism of the setting.

Elgar was not shocked. He was undoubtedly an English patriot from whatever perspective, and was completely unfazed by Benson's lyric, which in fact was neither a surprise nor unwelcome to him. It is true that the onset of WWI shocked him and he suggested less 'swaggering' words would be more appropriate. Elgar seems not, however, to have been as concerned about the human cost of the coming conflict as he was about the horses: 'Concerning the war I say nothing – the only thing that wrings my heart & soul is the thought of the horses – oh! my beloved animals – the men – and women can go to hell – but my horses; – I walk round & round this room cursing God for allowing dumb brutes to be tortured – let Him kill his human beings but how CAN HE? Oh, my horses' (more than 8 million horses were killed in the war).

The myth of Elgar storming out of a concert is, it turns out, a very recent creation, and is actually a scene from an obscure TV drama that has somehow become accepted as historical fact.

Andy Williams did not dub Lauren Bacall's singing voice in *To Have and Have Not*

The story that Andy Williams dubbed Lauren Bacall's voice when she sang the Hoagy Carmichael and Johnny Mercer song 'How Little We Know' in *To Have and Have Not* (1944) is quite appealing (Hoagy himself plays the pianist, Cricket, in the movie). The film critic Pauline Kael was one of the earliest promoters of the story, which has proved remarkably durable. Dubbing actors when they broke into song was commonplace in Hollywood and several very interesting singers (though not Jane Russell – another myth) were recorded and tried out for Bacall's singing voice, including the black singer Lillian Randolph (who later voiced the housekeeper in *Tom and Jerry* cartoons), and, indeed, Andy Williams.

Williams was born in 1927, and would have been all of 17 in 1944, perhaps not quite the right age to mimic Bacall's sultry contralto. But in any case, director Howard Hawks was so impressed with Bacall's version he kept it in. The singing voice you hear in the film is indeed hers.

Bacall and Humphrey Bogart share a joint myth, in that they are often believed to have suffered from a vocal disorder. There is in fact a 'vocal misuse disorder' called 'Bogart-Bacall Syndrome', a condition characterized by lisping in which the sufferer can experience vocal fatigue, but in fact neither star had this syndrome: it is just named after them because of their low-pitched film conversations.

George Formby was an anti-racist hero

George Formby's movies were popular in England and in the USSR but not elsewhere very much. In fact, though perhaps more watchable than Norman Wisdom movies, which were popular in England and Albania, they are extremely irritating, and when George gets amorous, a bit disturbing. *The Fast Show*'s 'Arthur Atkinson' character – with his ludicrous catchphrases and unfunny 'business' has made it very difficult to take the popular entertainers of Formby's generation seriously.

But in fact, as the playwright Dennis Potter kept insisting, British popular music from the 20s to the 40s was as good as any popular music anywhere, and Formby was a performer of some genius

His coy double entendres may be a minority taste nowadays, but he could entrance the demanding music hall audiences of his own day, even the fearsome Glasgow Empire.

In 1946 George and his wife Beryl (also his manager) flew to South Africa, Beryl as usual demanding the best of everything. The tour organisers were not sure how to promote George, and publicized him as 'the male Gracie Fields' (over 20,000 fans greeted them in Cape Town). The head of the National Party, Daniel Malan (who two years later would introduce apartheid), sent the Formbys a note telling them not to perform to coloured audiences. Beryl tore up the note and the Formbys declared war on the National Party, causing profound regime shock by playing 20 shows to black audiences. Though Beryl was famously mean, the Formbys took not a penny for the shows. Crisis came when a black child came on stage at one show and gave Beryl a box of chocolates: Beryl picked her up and kissed her, then passed her to George, who did the same, causing an immediate sensation. Next day Malan sent a delegation to give the Formbys a 'final warning', and the redoubtable Beryl slammed the door in their face. Malan then phoned Beryl and began to berate her. Beryl, at her most magnificent, simply said 'Why don't you piss off, you horrible little man?' and hung up. The Formbys were thrown out of South Africa.

They visited again in 1955 (Malan had served as prime minister 1948-54) and defied death threats to again perform before black audiences for free. The South African government was incensed, but there was little it could do but fume. The Formbys had fought the 'Beast' and won. Unfortunately, not many of the British performers who toured South Africa from then until the end of apartheid took the same defiant stand. The reactions of Malan showed how important such gestures could be.

Elvis Presley was not a racist

The slur that Elvis was a racist crops up from time to time, occasionally emanating from black writers and musicians, but more often from sad white men anxious to express both their solidarity with black culture and disdain for white exploiters of black traditions.

Not in so many words

"Crisis? What Crisis?" was the headline in *The Sun* on 11 January, 1979 above a picture of a smiling Prime Minister James Callaghan as he returned from a Caribbean summit conference to a cold and strike-bound Britain. In fact, when asked about his view of the "mounting chaos", he replied "I promise you that if you look at it from outside, and perhaps you're taking rather a parochial view at the moment, I don't think that other people in the world would share the view that there is mounting chaos."

In a sense, this is an issue not worth pursuing: the final proof of Presley's (quite startling for his time) lack of racial prejudice is in the absence of any accusations of it in Albert Goldman's much-reviled (by Elvis fans) biography, *Elvis* (1981). The book is painful reading for most Presley fans (it is actually horribly funny) but it seems clear to dispassionate readers that Goldman makes his case quite well: Presley may not have been the most likeable of human beings, but he was certainly not a racist.

The common form in which the accusation crops up is that sometime around 1957, Presley was in Boston (or perhaps on a TV show), and in the course of an interview he said, 'the only thing niggers can do for me is buy my records and shine my shoes'. There is, however, no evidence at all for this, and a wealth of testimony to the contrary from black performers who worked with Elvis, and indeed there is plenty of evidence that he took a stand against racism: to take one example among many, he refused to play the Houston Astrodome without his black backing singers.

The daftest charge against Presley is that he stole black songs, such as 'Hound Dog'. In fact 'Hound Dog' is one of many so-called 'black' songs that were actually written by New York Jews, in this case the great Lieber and Stoller (who continued a venerable Tin Pan Alley tradition of Jews writing authentic-sounding 'ethnic' songs; the 'Irish' and 'Scotch' songs their predecessors wrote being now performed as 'traditional' songs).

Mama Cass was not killed by a ham sandwich

'Mama' Cass Elliot (1941-1974) is well known as the 'large-framed' member of the 1960s vocal group 'The Mamas and the Papas'. An enduring myth holds that she choked to death on a sandwich. The sandwich is usually specified as containing ham, which is probably down to the usual accretion of specificity that occurs with urban myths – such stories become barnacle-encrusted with details that supposedly attest to their authenticity – but also perhaps subliminally suggests Cass was somehow 'piggy'.

It is sometimes additionally claimed that she 'really' died of a heroin overdose, or that she was having a child by John Lennon (or some other candidate). The truth is Mama Cass died of a heart attack, and the coroner's report explicitly states that no food was found in her trachea. She was unfit and overweight, indeed twice the weight she should have been; she was prone to starting 'quick result' diets, which are often themselves bad for your health and rarely do any good. Obesity killed Cass.

Another peculiar myth about Cass is that she was only allowed to join the Mamas and the Papas after a copper tube fell on her head (while the band was touring in the Virgin Islands), thus changing the pitch of her voice (and the history of human physiology) so that it exactly matched that of the founding female member of the band, Michelle Phillips. The Mamas and the Papas had many interpersonal issues, and it seems that this very odd story was started by a band member. Cass gave birth in 1967 to a daughter, Owen, and never named the father.

Cass died just after sell-out concerts at the London Palladium and, as is the way of things, was well on the way to becoming recognized as one of the great voices of her generation. She could duet with just about anybody, from Julie Andrews and Red Skelton, to Tom Jones and Johnny Cash. She died in Harry Nilsson's flat in Curzon Place, as did Keith Moon (*see **Keith Moon did not drive a Rolls-Royce into a swimming pool***).

Lionel Ritchie was not mistaken for a mugger in a lift by two old ladies

This is a classic example of urban myth. Two sweet and innocent old ladies go off to New York for a daring shopping weekend (one of them, no doubt, being the aunt of the person who told the person who is telling the story etc). Exhausted after a hard day in the stores, they enter a lift in their posh hotel, and are followed in by a tall black man with a large dog. The doors close, and the black man says 'Get down, lady'; the two women think they are being spoken to and go down on their knees, and plead with the black man not to hurt them.

The black man then apologises profusely and explains to the old ladies that he was talking to his dog, who is called Lady. Stricken by embarrassment and distress, the old ladies scuttle to their room and lock the door. Next morning they go to check out, and the person at the reception tells them that their bill has been paid (in some versions they also have a large bunch of flowers waiting for them). They say there must be some mistake, and they are told no, Mr Lionel Ritchie says it was the best laugh he has ever had.

The myth goes back at least to the mid-1980s, when it appeared in *The Spectator*. Indeed, it seems that the story reaches back even further, with Harry Belafonte playing the Ritchie part in the 60s, and perhaps Paul Robeson took the role even earlier! The story doubtlessly originates as a way of accommodating seemingly threatening (for white America) black men within a comforting narrative, and perhaps it is therefore not such a bad thing. It looks as if the first prominent male Muslim entertainer of the 21st century has an urban myth ready and waiting for him – all he needs is a dog called Lady...

Keith Moon did not drive a Rolls-Royce into a swimming pool

Keith Moon, drummer of The Who, died in 1978 aged 32. Dubbed 'Moon the Loon' he seems to have been mainly responsible for the hotel-wrecking image of The Who, and certainly engaged in wacky 'I am a rock star' antics. One of the famous, endlessly circulated stories about Moon is that he drove a Rolls-Royce into a swimming pool, though sometimes the car is said to be a Lincoln Continental. A fairly comprehensive biography by Tony Fletcher, *Moon:*

The Life and Death of A Rock Legend (1999), asserts that neither version is true: in fact, Moon at some point backed his Rolls-Royce into a pond, and from this rather dull event grew a thousand anecdotes. Fletcher deflates many myths about Moon in the course of his large and comprehensive book: he did not try to run over his own chauffeur either, for example.

Moon died in Harry Nilsson's flat in Curzon Place. He overdosed on a prescription drug he was taking to combat alcoholism, after watching *The Abominable Dr Phibes*. Mama Cass had died in the same flat four years previously (*see **Mama Cass was not killed by a ham sandwich***). Understandably spooked, Nilsson sold the flat (to an unspooked Pete Townshend).

Pink Floyd's *The Dark Side of the Moon* is not a 'soundtrack' for *The Wizard of Oz*

Of the many bizarre myths associated with rock music, one of the oddest is that the Pink Floyd album *The Dark Side of the Moon* (1973) is synchronized with the movie *The Wizard of Oz* (1939) as a soundtrack: the whole album is, in this view, a private joke.

Despite denials from band members such as Roger Waters – 'ridiculous. That's for people with too much free time' – the myth flourishes on many websites with scarily precise second-by-second analysis. But the creation of a 'concept' album such as *The Dark Side of the Moon* is a highly exacting collective work, requiring input from the musicians, engineers, guests and specialists and so forth. The killer answer to the myth is that if it were a private joke, then an awful lot of people would have had to have been in on it. Certainly the chief engineer, Alan Parsons, never heard the words 'Wizard of Oz' mentioned during the recording. Parsons also points out that synchronizing the album and its various elements with the film would have been a major technological feat requiring film projection in the studio – which just didn't happen.

It seems to be that humans are programmed to find synchronicity; it is part of what makes us human that we look for patterns and meanings. Thus if one is told that if the third roar of the MGM lion is synchronized with the beginning of the heartbeats that open *Dark Side*, then 'meanings' will emerge in the course of a viewing, meanings are what one will certainly find.

> ### Not in so many words
>
> "England expects that every man will do his duty," Nelson's signal to the fleet at Trafalgar has got the patriotic pulse of Englishmen going for two centuries. The original version of the message was the rather less stirring "Nelson confides that every man will do his duty", but he agreed to have "England" rather than "Nelson". The flag officer then found "expects" was quicker to signal than "confides".

John Lennon was a bit more materialistic than we imagine

Few of us may be perfect, but it has been a commonplace observation down the ages that those who tell the rest of us how to live should at least make some effort to be inspirational in their own mode of living. John Lennon's reputation as the great representative of 60s anti-materialism lives on, to the extent that many people still believe that when Lennon sang 'Imagine no possessions' his was a simple life of organic tofu and flower garlands.

In fact, Lennon's life included many material things. The most bizarre manifestation of this materialism was the room (some say apartment) he is said to have maintained at the Dakota building in Manhattan, stuffed with fur coats kept at a specially chilled temperature to keep them in good trim.

Was Lennon a teensy bit hypocritical, then? The answer seems obvious, though it could be argued that a lot depends on what you make of the song 'Imagine'. For many it is the best song of the 70s, hope and wisdom and peace all wrapped up in one; it is idealism at its purest, and has even been adopted as a socialist anthem. For others, 'Imagine' is the 'My Way' of the hippy generation, a maudlin, manipulative dirge coupled with a dismal, self-centred message.

The Lennon myth runs on, though probably not for much longer. Lennon himself is fading from public memory: an *Observer* poll of 2005 found that more Britons recognize Geri Halliwell than John Lennon, and the forgetting process seems to have speeded up. Twenty years ago it would have been unthinkable that a poll of top female singers could exclude Ella Fitzgerald and Peggy Lee, as such polls now often do. But then one remembers the conversation in James Joyce's story 'The Dead', with its lament for now forgotten singers: who now remembers Aunt Kate's 'sweet English tenor'? All gone, but such is the way of the world, and perhaps this is the really awful truth about John Lennon: our heroes fade to dust, as indeed will we all.

At least two members of the Village People were gay

A common pub quiz question is 'Which member of the Village People was really gay?', the answer being the Native American, Felipe Rosa (who was fond of claiming that he wasn't really dressing up, his costume being a celebration of his ethnic roots). Two members of the original line-up were actually gay, the other being Randy Jones (the cowboy). Jones left the group in 1980 and was replaced by Jeff Olsen. Olsen was not gay it seems, and neither, except for Rosa, were the other members of the group from 1980.

The Village People were formed in 1977, and can perhaps be described as the archetypal packaged pop group. They were arguably the first major pop group to emerge fully formed with marketing in mind. The Monkees were constructed from a bunch of mixed talent in 1966, but were a TV show first and foremost (*see **Charles Manson did not audition for the Monkees**)*; major groups such as the Beatles and Rolling Stones were often shaped by svengali-types, but also sourced from good musicians. The Village People were conceived and marketed as a novelty act from the outset.

Another common story about the Village People is that a senior member of the US Navy wanted to use 'In the Navy' as a recruiting song, until a junior officer explained the reality of the situation to him. In fact, the Navy helped the group with its video of the song, which was shot at San Diego naval base, with the Navy supplying a ship, planes and many personnel. A recruiting campaign actually began and used the song, but was quickly aborted when the press started drawing attention to the fact the US government was now funding pop videos (the sexuality issue seems to have been a relatively minor aspect in comparison).

Screen, Stage and TV

Walt Disney was not cryogenically frozen

Walt Disney was diagnosed with lung cancer in November 1966 and died a few weeks later in December. He was cremated and interred two days after his death at fabled Forest Lawn (the model for the 'Whispering Glades' in Evelyn Waugh's 1947 novel *The Loved One*). It has always been an efficient place, and it is as clear as can be that Disney was cremated there: it is a Forest Lawn embalmer whose signature is on the death certificate, and the Disney Estate paid $40,000 for his burial plot.

Despite the evidence, rumours began circulating shortly after his death that Walt Disney had been cryogenically frozen and his body would be hidden until science had progressed to the point where he could be brought back to life. The body, obviously, was stored somewhere in Disneyland, with the 'Pirates of the Caribbean' attraction being the favourite site (one of the pirate's faces is supposedly modelled on Disney and appeared after his death).

'Cryogenics' is defined by Chambers as 'the branch of physics concerned with phenomena at very low temperatures'; 'cryonics' is defined as 'the practice of preserving human corpses by freezing them, with the idea that advances in science may enable them to be revived at some future time'. Quite why the corpse of Walt Disney should be popularly believed to be in this state of 'cryonic suspension' is unclear. The answer is likely to lie with Disney's (and our own) obsession with the future…, with 'Tomorrowland'. Ever since Disneyland was invented, Disney's theme parks have been obsessed with showing us a future that keeps changing, but the future we were promised in the 1960s never happened; like Troy McClure's house in *The Simpsons*, Disney's 'Tomorrowland' is always showing us the future as it used to be.

At least two Disney biographies assert that Disney was interested in cryogenics, but it is not certain that he had even heard of the term. Perhaps we just like the irony of Disney being animated again.

Victor McLaglen was a British officer and not an Irish sergeant

From the 1930s through to the 1950s, Victor McLaglen (1883-1959) was the archetypal Irishman, particularly in John Ford westerns, such as *Fort Apache* (1948) and *She Wore a Yellow Ribbon* (1949). In fact, McLaglen was English, born in Tunbridge Wells, and his father was a clergyman who became an Anglican bishop in South Africa, where the young McLaglen tried to serve in the Boer War (1899-1902) by enlisting in the Life Guards (his father got him out). McLaglen wandered off to Canada where he became a professional prizefighter, and went six rounds with the legendary black heavyweight champion Jack Johnson in an exhibition fight in 1909 (a remarkable performance for a British boxer).

He enlisted at the outbreak of WWI, becoming a captain in the Royal Irish Fusiliers and – as Assistant Provost Marshal – joint ruler of Baghdad. After the war he acted in various British films, moved to Hollywood and won an Oscar in 1935 for his performance in John Ford's *The Informer*.

As writer George MacDonald Fraser points out, McLaglen's accent – whatever part he was called upon to play – was that of the old Victorian redcoat army: 'his voice never lost the clipped rasp of the old British Army, with its occasional "d" for "th", a voice with the authentic quality of the Victorian era'. The remarkable thing about McLaglen is that apart from being a very fine actor, he needed very little artifice to play a soldier whom Kipling would have recognized: he was the genuine article.

Ronald Reagan was not the original choice for Rick in *Casablanca*

This one often crops up in pub quizzes. The story that Humphrey Bogart only got the part of Rick in *Casablanca* after Ronald Reagan dropped out is untrue. The tale was made up by Warner Bros themselves in a press release that appeared in *The Hollywood Reporter* in January 1942. It also claimed that Ann Sheridan was to be the female lead, but no one took such press releases seriously in Hollywood – similar stories were frequently made up to keep stars' names in the press.

It is also very unlikely that George Raft (another commonly suggested 'original' Rick) was ever seriously considered for the role. Another well-known myth associated with the film, that Disney bought the actual plane featured at the end for its 'Great Movie Ride' in Disney World is untrue, as the Lockheeds used in the film are just props: smaller, but expertly scaled replicas. The film was mostly studio-bound. The mechanics pottering about the plane are actually little men ('midgets' it is said) who were hired to move about the mock-ups. It all looks very convincing thanks to the studio-produced fog. Eager myth-busters claim there is no fog in the real Casablanca, but this assertion itself is a myth: fog is by no means unknown in the real Casablanca, or of course anywhere else on the North African coast.

The story that Bogart had to stand on boxes during his scenes with Ingrid Bergman is very likely to be true: she was certainly taller than him. It does not seem to be true, however, that none of the actors knew how the film was going to end. A scenario in which Bogart flew off with Bergman was not just aesthetically unlikely, but hardly likely to be approved by a major studio: in those days, wives just didn't fly off with another man, leaving their heroic husbands behind, even if the other man was Bogie.

Lassie was a Yorkie (but not a bitch)

The original 'Lassie' book, *Lassie Come-Home*, was first published in 1938. The author, Eric Knight, was born in Yorkshire in 1897 and emigrated to the USA aged 15. Eric became a feature writer and also worked in Hollywood, but it was a trip back to 1930s Yorkshire – then in the grip of the Depression – that inspired the first Lassie book. The book's depiction of Yorkshire is rather grim: the life of the working people is hard, lung disease is common and families struggle to survive, selling their precious possessions to do so.

The collie Lassie is much loved by her young owner, Joe, but is reluctantly sold by Joe's father ('can't feed a dog on the dole') to the Duke of Rudling. She is sent to northern Scotland where she is brutally treated, but Lassie's affection for Joe remains strong. She runs away from the Duke's estate and travels south, growing weaker all the way, but of course finally makes it back to her Yorkshire homeland. The book is certainly sentimental, but the sentiment is grounded in the all too real dark presences of fear, want and loss, emotions that modern readers (in the west at least) are usually no longer as familiar with as the original audiences of the book and subsequent movies would have been. Knight was a good writer in command of his material, and *Lassie Come-Home* was quickly recognized as a classic of children's literature.

The first movie about Lassie, the unhyphenated *Lassie Come Home* (1943), can be a somewhat surreal experience for British viewers, as the movie's Scotland and Yorkshire were filmed in the USA, but it is a good solid melodrama. Roddy McDowell plays a tearfully effective Joe, especially at the school gate ('You're my Lassie come home!'), Nigel Bruce is a good gruff Duke, the young Elizabeth Taylor plays the Duke's kindly niece and Elsa Lanchester, Joe's mum, has some tough lines to handle: 'You might as well know it right off. Lassie won't be meeting you at school. She's been sold'. Lassie (who has pups at the end) is actually played by a male dog called Pal who was trained by the splendidly named Rudd Weatherwax, who deserves special note as he trained many succeeding Lassies in a string of films and TV shows.

Pal also played Lassie's son, Laddie, in *Son of Lassie* (1945), and is thus probably the only male lead in the movies to play a female, then be the female's son in the sequel. The film is rather good, as many of the 40s anti-Nazi Hollywood movies were, and there is surprisingly little attempt at anthropomorphism; Laddie is not blessed with the ability to recognize that men in Nazi uniforms are bad, for example. Joe is well played by future rat-pack member Peter Lawford.

Mr Ed was not a zebra

The story here is that Mr Ed, the talking horse star of the eponymous 1960s TV series, was not a horse at all, but a zebra.

It seems that this is a hoax started by the folk at the 'urban legends' site www.snopes.com, apparently in the hope of establishing how a hoax develops and spreads. It has spread pretty well; if you feel like wasting an hour of your life googling and yahooing you'll find quite a few people who accept this story as fact.

If you look at the 'lost legends' section on the Snopes site, you'll be informed that Mr Ed was not a horse but a zebra – a Grevy's zebra to be specific – and you'll find head shots of a zebra and Mr Ed to click between to show you what they each look like in colour and b&w. There is a lot of ancillary detail, like the set being scaled down to deal with zebras being smaller than horses, and fairly amusing stuff about prisoners supposedly escaping at Johnny Cash's Folsom prison concert (they were wearing black and white and were therefore invisible on the TV monitors) and so forth.

Snopes's point is, of course, that you should be sceptical about all your sources, including Snopes (and also, of course, this book).

Not everyone thought David Niven was the perfect gentleman

During and after WWII a succession of British actors received awards – knighthoods, CBEs, MBEs, etc, from a grateful British government (making new dames out of old queens, as one wag put it). The honours were based on a wide variety of contributions to the Allied war effort, whether raising money, making speeches, starring in ropy propaganda films to bolster morale or to persuade a reluctant USA that the Brits were worth fighting for. Some of the honours even went to actors who'd put in some actual front-line war service.

It's all the more puzzling then, that David Niven – widely seen as the screen's quintessential English gentleman – should have been passed over. It is true that few of his films were masterpieces (with a few glorious exceptions, such as the 1946 *A Matter of Life and Death*). But quality of work wasn't a factor in official recognition. And above all Niven showed he meant business by returning to Britain from Hollywood and enlisting, ending up as a commando officer.

After Niven's death in 1983, the customary journalistic hounds were dispatched to dig the dirt on the man; no one ever came up with anything very much. Niven was largely what he seemed, a kind family man, a patriot, and a participant in a few movies that will live as long as cinema lives. When his own papers became available for biographical research, it became evident he was not perfect: he had frequent affairs, he wasn't always truthful, yet, for a Hollywood figure, he was practically a saint.

Why then was David Niven never honoured by the British government when much lesser talents (some with much bigger and bonier skeletons in their closets) had honours heaped upon them? A recurring theory is based on an alleged friendship with Prince Philip. Lauren Bacall indicated to Graham Lord, author of *Niv: The Authorised Biography of David Niven* (2003), that Philip used Niven as a 'beard'; in this scenario, Philip could appear with his girlfriends in public with the actor, with the pretence that the girls belonged to Niven. If this did happen, it could be that there was a fall-out in the course of this arrangement, the consequence being that Niven was blacklisted in some way by the British establishment.

Niven's wit and talent must certainly have earned him enemies, and he was capable of delivering deadly thrusts with the 'too kind' charm he was so good at. Perhaps Niven simply skewered one influential person too many, but the puzzle of the lack of official recognition for his sterling war service remains a genuine mystery.

> ### Not in so many words
>
> "Father, I cannot tell a lie. I did it with my little hatchet." George Washington as a child is supposed to have confessed this to his father after chopping down a small cherry tree. However, the story was invented by Parson Weems in his biography of Washington, published in 1800 just after the president's death. Weems also claims the angels felt "fresh raptures" when Washington went to heaven, a marginally less reliable anecdote.

Marlon Brando did not ride a Harley-Davidson in *The Wild One*

The most miscaptioned movie still of all time is probably the famous Brando pic for *The Wild One* (1953), a head-on shot of the man looking over the handlebars of his bike, hat set at a jaunty angle, looking ridiculously cool (or perhaps just a little camp). The bike is quite clearly a Triumph – it even says Triumph on the bike – and *The Wild One* is apparently the first Hollywood film in which a motorcycle's tank badge is on open display. The bike itself is a 1950

Thunderbird. Yet when the photograph is reproduced in a newspaper or magazine, the picture will almost inevitably be captioned 'Brando with Harley' (Lee Marvin does ride a Harley in the film, and with some delicacy; he took a Japanese bullet in the bum during WWII).

Whatever an icon may be, Brando seems unquestionably to fit the bill, as does the Harley-Davidson motorcycle; so if Brando is pictured with a bike, the bike must therefore be a Harley in the condensed world of caption writing, despite the awesome counterweight of Hollywood precedent: James Dean owned a Triumph with 'Dean's Dilemma' on the side, Clint Eastwood rode a Triumph Bonneville through Central Park in *Coogan's Bluff* (1968), Richard Gere has a Bonnie in *An Officer and a Gentleman* (1982) and the greatest Triumph movie scene of them all is 'Cooler King' Steve McQueen in *The Great Escape* (1963), almost managing to leap across the barbed wire barriers at the Swiss border (on a wildly anachronistic 1960s model, not that it matters).

With that sort of record, how did British bikes become uncool? The theory is that British bike makers such as Triumph and BSA sneered at Japanese bikes when they first emerged and ignored market indicators that consumers would like sexy colours. The British would only supply in black (echoing the Henry Ford myth: *see **Henry Ford did cars in green with a red stripe***), while the Japanese sprayed their bikes in garish colours and the world was never the same again. It's a good story with an obvious moral, but the truth is probably a bit more complex...

Jerry Lewis is not universally loved in France

It is commonly believed in Anglophone countries that Jerry Lewis is idolized by French film critics. This goes pretty well with the British and American supposition that the French take things a bit too seriously when it comes to films.

In fact, most contemporary French people are no more aware of Jerry Lewis than Brits and Americans are – he's the dim half of an old double act that made some pretty mediocre films in the 1950s and 1960s. Lewis was indeed in vogue among French intellectual circles for a while, but as a director. His films, such as *The Ladies Man* (1961) and *The Nutty Professor* (1963), covered similar themes, which fitted well with the 'auteur' theory that was popular with the influential magazine *Cahiers du Cinema*. With auteur theory, it certainly helped if you were good, but consistency was better. Most people would say that John Huston was a more important director than Lewis, but the latter's films can satisfactorily be studied as a coherent 'oeuvre', while Huston's films are startlingly different from each other.

It has been suggested that Lewis, as a performer, appealed to a specifically French tradition of comic monologues done with grimaces and freakish facial tics. Rae Beth Gordon, in her *Why the French Love Jerry Lewis* (2001), argues that French cafe traditions of epileptic singers and 'idiot comics' created fertile ground for a comedian such as Lewis in France. If so, when Lewis first became known in France he was probably appealing to the tail end of a tradition, and not one which has a lot of influence on today's French cinemagoers, or critics.

One of Lewis's films does stand completely outside his normal work (indeed, it may be unlike any other film ever made by anyone), *The Day the Clown Cried* (1971). The film tells the story of a German clown whose job it is to march children to the gas chambers in a Nazi death camp, and has been the subject of both litigation and much speculation. It certainly shows Lewis determined to break new ground, but it has only been seen by a handful of people, and may never be released.

Hitchcock did direct the shower scene in *Psycho*

The story that Alfred Hitchcock did not direct the 'shower scene' in the classic horror film *Psycho* (1960) is not true, despite frequent assertions that the film's brilliant designer Saul Bass was responsible. It is a myth that has been given credence by Leslie Halliwell, among others. Bass (who died in 1996 and is regarded as one of the greatest graphic designers of the 1950s) seemingly did a meticulous storyboard for this complex scene, which includes over 90 'splices'. But the crucial evidence for Hitchcock is the testimony of the actress Janet Leigh, who dies so scarily in the scene. Interviewed in 1999 for *Literature Film Quarterly*, Leigh became quite irate when the story that Bass directed the scene was put to her. She asserted: 'Sam Bass did not direct the shower scene, and I told him to his face, how dare he say that?' Leigh says that Hitchcock missed one day during filming when he had flu but it was not the shower scene. And when he came back he re-shot a scene (of Martin Balsam going up the stairs) which had been filmed in his absence by his assistant director, 'because it wasn't right'. Leigh adds that the assistant director, Hilton Green, also got upset by suggestions that Bass directed the scene.

There is a counter-theory for the Bass case that perhaps has a certain degree of credibility. This is the belief that a few days before the filming of the shower scene, Bass filmed (with a newsreel camera) Janet Leigh's stand-in in the shower, but did so outside of normal production hours. The theory is that some of this footage was subsequently used in the movie. However, if such an event took place it's entirely possible that the film wasn't intended for public consumption…

The myth may have begun with a 1973 *Sunday Times* interview in which the interviewer simply misunderstood what Bass was saying. Bass never seems to have quite claimed that he did, for certain, direct the shower scene. Perhaps he was simply content to let rest unchallenged the impression that he may have directed one of the greatest scenes in the history of film.

Not a lot of people know this about Michael Caine…

Michael Caine is now forever identified with the words 'My name is Michael Caine' and the catchphrase 'Not a lot of people know that'. The latter expression is an essential element in any Caine impression, spoken in a distinctive 'mockney' accent.

Caine has been much imitated throughout his career. His voice is both highly singular yet easy to pastiche, and there is a fair degree of affection in the imitation: people like Michael Caine.

The phrase, however, is not his. Peters Sellers claimed to have originated it in a telephone answering message saying: 'My name is Michael Caine. Peter Sellers is not in at the moment. Not a lot of people know that.' Peter Sellers was prone to inventing stories, but this one seems true. Certainly no one has identified Caine himself using the quote except in a self-mocking spirit.

This is not the only case of an impressionist's invention being adopted by a good-natured 'victim'. Television impressionist Mike Yarwood used to do an impression of the Labour Chancellor of the Exchequer Denis Healey that generally featured the words 'Silly Billy'. Healey subsequently began to use the catchphrase himself, like Caine, in a humorous spirit, and it has since been attributed to him.

In 1984, Michael Caine spoke on the Madness song 'Michael Caine', his contributions being 'I am Michael Caine' (twice) and 'My name is Michael Caine' (twice). Caine thus became one of the very few people to guest on a hit song (it reached number 11 in the UK chart) named after himself.

There were no doughnuts like Fanny's

In British TV cookery, there is BC and AD: Before Cradock, and After Delia. Cradock (not 'Craddock') was the very first celebrity TV chef and always appeared with her dithering 'husband' Johnnie (though they did not in fact marry until 1977 – a very well-kept secret). Many people claim to have heard Johnnie Cradock say at the end of one of their cookery programmes, 'And I hope all your doughnuts turn out like Fanny's' or perhaps 'Great cooking is making doughnuts like Fanny's'. There is, alas, no authoritative record of the quotation, which has also been attributed to David Coleman and Frank Bough.

The doughnut quote is apocryphal, but the popular memory of a double act that seems in retrospect even more bizarre than the recipes is not exaggerated. The Cradock's show ran on BBC television from the mid-1950s to (incredibly) the mid-1970s, by which time both the Cradocks and their recipes were constantly ridiculed and parodied. The era of recipes that called for gelatine in electric colours had long passed.

The defining moment in Fanny's slide to oblivion came on her live TV show when she turned on a nice lady who was rash enough to express an opinion Fanny didn't agree with (this embarrassing moment turns up frequently on clips shows). She was a terrible, but also honest, snob who saw no reason to hide her disdain for common people and their common little ways. On one memorable occasion she recommended a recipe to 'lonely old people', which was perhaps insensitive but also filled a need: lonely old people exist and no doubt need helpful recipes.

She also wrote four novels, including, surprisingly, two science fiction 'lost race' tales about a decadent Atlantis. She published these as Phyllis (her real first name) Cradock. Her maiden name was Primrose-Peachy.

Rod Stewart did not try to buy up every copy of *The Wicker Man*

The movie *The Wicker Man* (1973) has become a 'cult' classic, that is to say a movie, good or bad, which somehow succeeds in becoming more than the sum of its parts and acquires a dedicated following who study and celebrate the film. Indeed, in this particular case, the movie has even spawned a folkish music festival designed to celebrate the supposed old druid religion (though without, one supposes, burning any members of the local constabulary).

The movie has spawned lots of myths and rumours, including the frequent assertion that Rod Stewart was so disturbed at the thought of cinemagoers seeing his then girlfriend Britt Ekland's naked body, that he tried to buy up every copy of the film. This is not true, and in any case Ekland had a body double for some of the more exposed scenes, so you don't really see much of the real Britt. You don't actually hear her singing voice either, as this was dubbed with the voice of the Scots jazz singer Annie Ross. There are lots of iconic figures in the film, including Christopher Lee, the mime artist Lindsay Kemp and Ingrid Pitt (valiantly playing a Scottish librarian). Lee is apparently largely responsible for rescuing the film from oblivion, when he referred to it in an interview as his best work.

The various rituals in the film are a blend of hippie smoke, Hammer horror and fusty Victorian theories of druidism derived from Sir James Frazer's *The Golden Bough*. No one actually knows what druidism was really about, but it almost certainly involved human sacrifice, and who is to say that a real druid priest would not have found the burning at the end authentic?

The final shots of the film are stunning and were achieved thanks to a fortuitous break in the weather. The story that Edward Woodward was peed on by a frightened goat during the filming is apparently true. There are stories that some of the animals in the Wicker Man died, but this remains unconfirmed.

Not in so many words

"Houston, we have a problem." The actual message from the Apollo 13 astronaut Jack Swigert to Mission Control in 1970 was not (quite) so terse: "Okay, Houston, we've had a problem here". His fellow astronaut Jim Lovell added "Houston, we've had a problem".

There is no Master Bates in *Captain Pugwash* (and no Seaman Staines)

Legends about children's television programmes seem to be present in all countries where children have grown up watching television. Perhaps this is truer of Britain than most countries, partly because the quality of our children's television has been high, and partly because we do like to reminisce, even about trivia like Andy Pandy or Trumpton.

Captain Pugwash had a very long career in print from the early 1950s onwards, and first appeared on telly in 1957, with the last series coming along in 1975, by which time Pugwash had become firmly lodged in the popular consciousness. A persistent legend about the series has it that several of the characters had sexually suggestive names: the two most common references are to Master Bates and Seaman Staines, with 'Roger the Cabin Boy' a frequent addition. It has also been suggested that 'Pugwash' is a euphemism for oral sex.

There are, of course, no such characters anywhere in the series, and the name Pugwash was taken from a town in Nova Scotia. The crew of the *Black Pig* comprised Master Mate, Tom the Cabin Boy, and the pirates Barnabas and Willy. How the fable about the non-existent characters started is not known (there are various claimants), but may have begun soon after the series ended in 1975. In 1991 the series creator, John Ryan, got a retraction and fulsome apology, with damages and costs from *The Guardian*, after it printed the story as fact.

There have been one or two fictional characters elsewhere who carry names that sail a bit close to the wind: a 'Roger the Cabin Boy' appears in Arthur Ransome's classic *Swallows and Amazons* (1930), and the TV series *The Onedin Line* (1971) had a character called 'Mister Baines'.

There are no subliminal porn scenes in Disney movies

Given Disney's position in American and world culture as a provider of family entertainment it is perhaps inevitable that rumours should arise about subliminal porn scenes and similar nasties in the company's films.

Some startling stories about Disney Studios turn out to be true (*see **Lemmings do not leap off cliffs***) but despite a great deal of misspent study, the only firm (as it were) sexual reference is in the 1992 video release of *The Rescuers* (1977), in which a topless woman appears at a window as Bianca and Beatrice fly past. The image appears twice and so briefly it would be impossible to see the images unless you freeze each frame. Disney recalled over 3 million copies of the video despite the fact that no viewer seems to have noticed – Disney take their family image that seriously.

That case apart, the spotting of subliminal sexual messages in Disney movies perhaps says more about the spotter than the film. Popular Internet claims include: that the word 'SEX' appears in a dust cloud in *The Lion King*; that there is a scene in *Aladdin* telling children to take off their clothes; that someone has an erection during the wedding scene in *The Little Mermaid*, and so on. The usual story is that a disgruntled employee is responsible for the supposed sexual element, but given the collaborative nature of cartoon work it is unlikely such a feat could ever be managed (*The Rescuers* coup is assumed to have been achieved during post-production).

As *The Rescuers* shows, it is in fact not impossible for a sexual reference to get through in the cartoon world: there are several sexual references in *The Simpsons*: a joke by Krusty about a 12-inch pianist, for example, but the creative environments of Disney and *The Simpsons* are totally different.

One of the most famous examples of a hidden sex scene – indeed of several sex scenes – is on a 1970s Huntley & Palmers biscuit tin. This was the work of a disgruntled employee (in Liverpool) and is now very collectable. The tin depicts a very busy faux-Regency scene in the grounds of a manor house, and includes in the background two dogs coupling, and a man and a woman having sex in a flower-bed. There is also a jam jar with a dubious label. The tin is known throughout the antiques trade as 'The Disgruntled Employee Biscuit Tin'.

Benny Hill never said how sad he was at Frankie Howerd's death

The comedian Frankie Howerd (born Howard) died of heart failure on 19 April 1992. By the time he died he had become a major cult figure in British comedy, having appeared in everything from the *Carry On* films to Shakespearian comedy and satire such as *That Was the Week That Was*. His television show *Up Pompeii* (1969), with its bawdy mix of double entendres and fruity asides to the viewers, established him as a great favourite with British audiences.

His career path was not dissimilar to that of Benny Hill's, though the latter found more worldwide appeal with his now seemingly immortal TV shows (at any given time, some broadcaster somewhere is probably showing *The Benny Hill Show*). Comedians are traditionally supposed to be miserable, but both Howerd and Hill were unhappy in their personal lives: Howerd was gay, with a reputation for propositioning startled young men, while Hill's sex life is pretty obscure, perhaps thankfully. They both suffered terribly from stage fright, Howerd's trademark stammer being a direct result of years of fear at having to face an audience.

Howerd's death was not unexpected. He was admitted to hospital with respiratory problems, and his heart gave out shortly after a visit from his old friend Cilla Black. The tributes flowed in. Howerd was an exceptional talent, as his peers were ready to testify. Among those asked for a comment was Benny Hill. Those who phoned Benny's house got no answer so his agent made up a quote describing how sad Benny was at Frankie Howerd's death, a great loss, etc., and Benny's farewell to Frankie featured in the media on 20 April.

But Benny himself was dying, seated in his favourite chair in front of the telly, and died on the 20th, as the nation read his supposed tribute to Frankie (it is sometimes said he actually predeceased Frankie, but this seems unlikely).

On 24 April, his door was broken down and the body was discovered. He left a huge fortune and much financial confusion. Not long after he died, a rumour spread that he had been buried with a large amount of gold, and his coffin was broken into by grave robbers.

There were no bodhrans on the *Titanic*

James Cameron's film *Titanic* was one of the most successful films ever made. It also has a tiresomely familiar racist subtext: the English are portrayed as cowardly snobs (though at least one of the chief English creeps in the film was actually a Scot), while the immigrants in steerage, notably the Irish and Italians, are all merry, democratic Americans in embryo. The contrast is emphasized when DiCaprio takes Winslet down below to the joyful Irish dancing, with the bodhran – a goatskin framed drum – banging mercilessly away.

That bodhran's presence is, however, anachronistic. Irish music historians have engaged in a lot of pondering of old photographs, and ears have been much bent to listen to archive recordings, but in truth the bodhran seems to have emerged fully fledged in the 1960s (some say as precisely as 1962), when bands such as The Chieftains began using it. There is certainly no firm evidence for its existence prior to the 1960s. The Irish musicologist Ronan Nolan has wittily suggested it was possibly invented by Kerry farmers to push up the price of goatskin, but it could also just be a tambourine with its bells taped up (it seems at least plausible that the word 'bodhran' has developed from the contraction 'bourine').

There's an even more intriguing solution to the origin of the instrument: perhaps this supposedly Celtic instrument is actually English in origin, and is a version of the West Country 'riddle drum' which made the short migration to Ireland in the 1960s. Whatever the instrument's exact origin, it looks as if the bodhran-bangers on Dublin's O'Connell St are less rooted in Celtic tradition than concert recitals of Beethoven's Scottish and Irish songs.

It is unscientific to use scientists in adverts

There is a minority but persistent belief in the advertising industry that using scientists in adverts will impress the punters. This is an example of one of those curious fallacies that is clung to by some people within a profession, often to the bafflement of their peers as well as to outsiders. In fact, there is no evidence at all that, for example, using Stephen Hawking to advertise a credit fund will inspire people to invest in that fund. It may even be counter-productive.

Using real and well-known scientists in adverts has always been a contentious practice. The target markets are now quite rightly suspicious of scientists telling them 'buy this product', even if, as Hawking does in one ad, he is circling the globe in a wheelchair. Until the 1960s, cigarette advertising for particular brands would often portray avuncular actors in white coats and stethoscopes talking lyrically about the positive medical effects of smoking this or that particular brand. Real scientists and doctors were sometimes used, but then those were the days when real doctors could recommend smoking to their patients as lung exercise.

Celebrities are a different matter. In a well-known cosmetics advert, the *Friends* star Jennifer Aniston famously tells the viewer 'here comes the science bit'. It sticks with people because the advert exploits first of all the celebrity image of Aniston herself, then moves on to the boring but 'true' science part of the advert. The viewer sees the ploy but accepts it as a good joke. The thing is done with intelligence, even grace.

But using real scientists can encourage derision and is often risky for the product's image. For example, a 1998 Renault advert used the geneticist Steve Jones to endorse a Renault car – yet as an *Economist* review of the campaign pointed out, science teaches that evolution certainly means change, but not necessarily what we would call 'progress', and the idea of progress is exactly what Renault wants people to take from the advert.

Incidentally, Jennifer Aniston has herself become a 'science bit'. It has been suggested that our brain becomes 'wired' to recognize members of our family or people we see regularly at work or even on television. The neurons that fire up on recognition have been dubbed 'Jennifer Aniston cells' (also called 'grandmother cells'). But then this might just be a case of scientists doing a bit of advertising themselves – drumming up publicity for an interesting, but hardly earth-shattering discovery, by hitching it to the name of a celebrity.

Director's cuts are not the definitive version

In an episode of *The Simpsons*, Homer is sitting in a hotel room watching *Free Willy* ('free food... Free Willy!'). At the end of the film Willy fails to jump over the little boy into the open sea; in fact he falls on top of the unfortunate child. Homer is aghast and exclaims 'Oh, I don't like this new director's cut!'.

Homer is not alone. Indeed, with the proliferation of director's cuts since the invention of the DVD, Homer's disillusionment is becoming common, but with hope triumphing over experience, most people still think that director's cuts are likely to be an improvement on the original version. But for every improvement, like *Blade Runner* (though even this is contentious – some of us liked the voice-over narration), there are dozens like *Donnie Darko*, where the new version causes deep dismay to many admirers of the original film.

The director's cut is now basically a marketing exercise to offer the manufacturer a second bite at the market under the guise of giving the purchaser the chance to share the director's true vision, which in practice may just mean more of the most annoying bits – you could call it the 'extra ewoks effect' in the case of *Star Wars*.

The extent to which cinema is a collective or individual art form is much debated. Believers in auteur theory will see the director as a poet like Shakespeare; dissenters like Gore Vidal see the director as a useful but marginal operator, the 'brother-in-law'. Movie fans are lucky that DVDs did not come earlier. A great movie such as John Ford's *The Searchers* (1956) is the work of a fine director to be sure, but the script and cinematography are from other individuals. A director's cut of *The Searchers* would probably not have added better words or camerawork – what you might well have got is more of Ford's tiresome hokum and horseplay.

The Peckinpah film about the Lincoln County War, *Pat Garrett and Billy the Kid* (1973), has its flaws but is a fine and dark riposte to the John Wayne movie, *Chisum* (1970), in which Wayne plays the eponymous hero as a benevolent capitalist giant protecting white America and its minorities. In the Peckinpah film, Chisum is still symbolic of America, but it is a brutal and exploitative country. In the director's cut you get extra killing of course, this being Peckinpah, but you also get Chisum himself on screen, which is rather irritating. In the original shortened version, Chisum does not appear, allowing the viewer to picture Wayne in the role. The original cut of the movie works better in every way.

Not in so many words

"Lead on, Macduff." This phrase is sometimes used as an invitation to allow another to take the lead. The original is in fact a challenge to final, mortal combat, as Macbeth says: "Lay on, Macduff, And damned be him that first cries 'Hold, enough!'"

Star Trek may not be as racially progressive as you might think

There are plenty of odd things about the many series of *Star Trek* but it has always had a well-deserved name for promoting understanding between nations and races. The original series had a (fairly) prominent Russian crew member in *Enterprise* navigator Pavel Chekov, even though US-Soviet relations were then (1966-69) still distinctly chilly. Even more significantly, what seems to have been the first black/white kiss on a US national TV series took place when Captain Kirk kissed Lt Uhuru (whose name, of course, is Swahili for 'freedom'). It seems surprising therefore, to find anyone claiming that *Star Trek* might be tinged with anti-semitism.

No one has suggested that Gene Roddenberry, the series' creator, was in any way anti-semitic, but it has been argued that the Ferengi traders in *Star Trek* appear to draw upon a wealth of anti-semitic caricatures embedded in western culture. In fact, the Ferengi were created not by Roddenberry himself but by Herbert J Wright (the 'Father of the Ferengi', as trekkies call him; he died in 2005), and their first appearance was in 'The Last Outpost', a 1987 episode of

Star Trek: the Next Generation. They were apparently intended to re-place Klingons as Federation enemies, but even *Star Trek* fans found them too ridiculous in appearance to be menacing.

Who are the Ferengi? They are a wandering race who live in exile from their homeland: they are squat and shifty, and have good 'lobes' for business (their huge ears could be seen as an equivalent to huge noses). They walk in an odd shambling manner, are crafty rather than intelligent, and constantly seek to accumulate wealth. They are merchants who wear distinctive clothing; they engage in money-lending, and have a yen for human women.

'Ferengi', as it happens, is Farsi for foreigner and has spread to other languages such as Urdu. Perhaps, then, those who draw parallels be-tween *Star Trek*'s Ferengi and western racist stereotypes of Jews are missing the point, and the wily merchants are really meant to stand for every kind of despised outsider.

The USA, Past and Present

The US Founding Fathers were not too keen on freedom and democracy

'How is it that we hear the loudest yelps for liberty among the drivers of negroes?': Dr Johnson's question about the American Revolutionaries has only rarely been addressed in America, where the name of Crispus Attucks – the slave who was shot by the British during the 'Boston Massacre' of 1770 – is known to every schoolchild, but the names of loyalist African-Americans such as Thomas Peters are practically unknown; as is the fact that reports of challenges to slavery under English law on English soil spread rapidly among American slaves who fully realized the implication for the British colonies in America. The slaveholders who made the American Revolution in 1776 knew that continued British rule would mean the end of slavery. As Simon Schama has said, behind the white mask of the American Revolution is the 'great American slave uprising', a forgotten mass war of slaves against their white American masters.

Thomas Jefferson is often held up as an example of a Founding Father who cared about enslaved blacks and would have liked to emancipate them, but the evidence for this is unclear. When Jefferson wrote 'never yet could I find that a black had uttered a thought above the level of plain narration', he was doubtless expressing a liberal American view, but a view that British conservatives such as Dr Johnson found repellent, irrational and un-Christian.

Very little of this is known to modern Americans. In that ludicrous movie, *The Patriot*, many white American audiences doubtless believe they are watching historical fact when the character played by Mel Gibson takes leave of his black 'employees' who wish him well in fighting the British oppressor (Gibson changed the name of the character he was playing when historians pointed out that his original, General Francis Marion, the so-called 'Swamp Fox', raped his slaves and killed Native Americans for fun).

But it wasn't just blacks or Native Americans that the American ruling class didn't care for: they didn't like their fellow whites either. The Revolution was imposed from above, with John Adams surmising that only a third of white Americans were in favour (add blacks and Native Americans, and one gets a *huge* all-race majority against the Revolution). The Founding Fathers often expressed their fear of democracy and the 'common man'. As historian Charles Beard points out, most of the drafters of the American Constitution regarded democracy 'as something rather to be dreaded than encouraged'.

Nor were the winners gracious in victory: the treatment of Loyalists after the Revolution was appalling, and the émigré rate was much higher than that for the subsequent French Revolution. The American Terror remains one of history's dark corners.

There is no hard evidence that Betsy Ross sewed the first American flag

Here's the story. Betsy Ross (née Griscom) was the 8th of 17 children of a Philadelphia Quaker family which disowned her after she eloped with John Ross, an episcopalian. The couple ran an upholstery business together, but John died in a gunpowder explosion in 1776. In June of that year Betsy was supposedly visited by George Washington and two other Congress members, and asked to design a flag. This she did, sewing the flag in her humble parlour; there is a splendid painting of Betsy presenting the finished article to a suitably impressed George Washington (who had done an initial briefing sketch for Betsy, revised at Betsy's suggestion).

This lovely scenario, however, only became public long after the deaths of the individuals concerned. In 1870 (that's 94 years after the event), Betsy's grandson, William Canby, presented a paper to the Historical Society of Pennsylvania revealing for the first time the Ross family account, an account bolstered by sworn affidavits from Betsy's daughter and other family members. However, there is not a scrap of contemporary evidence for the story, though, as is the way with such stories, 'evidence' began to accumulate on the Betsy side, and now her old house is a fine museum. The Betsy website says she is one of the 'most cherished figures of American history', which is very likely true, always bearing in mind the lines from John Ford's movie *The Man Who Shot Liberty Valence*: 'when the legend becomes fact, print the legend.'

One of the anti-Betsy schools of history claims that the flag was actually designed by Francis Hopkinson, a member of Congress and signer of the Declaration of Independence. But at this late date it seems that no one will ever know for sure.

Uncle Tom was not an 'Uncle Tom'

The expression 'Uncle Tom', used to denote a black man who is in theory free but is still subservient to whites (female Uncle Toms are called Aunt Jemimas), is a reference of course to *Uncle Tom's Cabin* (1852), the novel by Harriet Beecher Stowe that has been regarded by many, including Abraham Lincoln, as the spark that started the American Civil War. It is one of those rare books that people think they know even if they haven't read it. It is a masterpiece: cleverly written and uncompromising in its view of slavery. Stowe refused to trim her sails for those who argued there were 'good' slave owners. At one point, when a Southerner nervously hopes that a Northern observer will not think that the brutal Simon Legree is typical of slave owners, the Northerner observes that, on the contrary, it is the supposedly decent slave owners who are the problem: if all were like Legree the façade would be stripped away and the system would collapse. The often nightmarish Cruikshank illustrations in the British edition (also 1852) complement Stowe's text especially well, his portrayal of Emmeline on the auction block surrounded by eager bidders being the perfect visualization of the dark sexual reality of slavery.

The book was phenomenally successful, selling over 2 million copies by 1860. Slavery sympathizers threw their own fiction into the propaganda war, including the memorably titled *Uncle Robin in His Cabin in Virginia, And Tom Without One in Boston* (1853), which showed Tom dying a miserable free man and Robin dying a happy Christian slave (slave-owning Christians and Muslims have always emphasized how slavery benefited blacks by bringing them true religion; indeed this point of view is still very much alive in Arab North Africa). But the competing works – divorced as they were from any reality – are long-forgotten, except by historians.

As several critics have observed, Tom's quiet dignity ('I'd rather have poor clothes, poor house, poor everything and have 'em mine, than have the best, and have 'em any man else's') is not that passive, and could be seen as a foreshadowing of Gandhi's later principle of non-violent resistance.

Chief Seattle's great ecological speech of 1854 was actually written in 1971 by a Texan screenwriter

Chief Seattle was a Squamish chief in what is now Washington state; in 1854 he gave a speech in which he addressed the new territorial governor, Isaac Stevens, who wanted the Squamish to sign away their lands for white settlers. We can say with a fair degree of certainty that Seattle did not respond with joy to this request but beyond that even the first reported version of the speech gives us problems. There are in fact several versions of the speech.

The first (1887) is the only one with even a remote claim to authenticity. A Dr Henry Smith, described by a contemporary as a 'poet of no ordinary talent', took some notes on the speech which he wrote up 33 years later for publication in the Seattle *Sunday Star* (29/10/1887). It is a fine example of flowery high Victorian – 'My people are few. They resemble the scattering trees of a storm-swept plain. The great, and I presume – good, White Chief' and much more in this vein. This 'original version' may even be third-hand, as Seattle's own language may have been translated into Chinook first.

The second is a classic document from the late 1960s by the poet William Arrowsmith and is much removed from anything Seattle might have said. It sounds like a Joni Mitchell pastiche: 'Your God is prejudiced. He came to the white man. We never saw him, never even heard his voice. He gave the white man laws, but he had no word for his red children whose numbers once filled this land as the stars filled the sky.'

The third and most famous version is by the Texan writer Ted Perry. This is the text that still hangs upon thousands of student walls and was described by a leading British churchman as the 'fifth gospel'. It includes this ecological gem: 'I've seen a thousand rotting buffaloes on the prairie, left by the white man who shot them from a passing train' – though it is highly unlikely that Seattle ever saw a buffalo, and he would certainly never have seen a train. Ted Perry himself seemed a bit embarrassed by it all: as he later said, he hadn't 'the slightest knowledge of Indian views on the environment'. And it's not just Seattle's words that have been tampered with – as a 1992 *Newsweek* piece pointed out, even his photograph has been altered to open his eyes, and in one reproduction his head has been put on a more myth-friendly body.

Little Tree was no Cherokee

*T*he *Education of Little Tree* (1976) was published and marketed as the autobiography of Little Tree, a part-Cherokee orphan who rediscovers his true roots from his in-touch-with-nature Native American grandparents. The publisher's blurb on Amazon says the story 'has entranced readers of all ages since it was first published twenty-five years ago... "Little Tree", as his grandparents call him, is shown how to hunt and survive in the mountains, to respect nature in the Cherokee Way, taking only what is needed, leaving the rest for nature to run its course'.

The so-called 'Cherokee Way' is contrasted with the grasping materialism of the dominant white culture. The authenticity of the book – which is very popular and has sold well over half a million copies – was never questioned until 12 years after the death in 1979 of the actual author, Forrest Carter.

The book is pure fiction and Forrest Carter's real name was Asa Earl Carter – the adopted first name 'Forrest' was chosen in honour of the founder of the Ku Klux Klan, Nathan Bedford Forrest. Carter probably had no Native American ancestry, and was a white supremacist who wrote speeches for George Wallace (*see **The Gov'nor is not loved by all in Birmingham***). His best-known contribution to American rhetoric, after *The Education of Little Tree*, is Wallace's slogan 'Segregation now! Segregation tomorrow! Segregation forever!'. Relations between Carter and Wallace deteriorated after Carter ran against him in a 1970 election, claiming he had gone soft.

Carter was a violent man (his death may have been the result of a fist fight with one of his own sons), and has been described, plausibly enough, as a psychopath. Back in the 1950s he had helped form a breakaway group from the KKK, among the least gruesome exploits of which was assaulting the black singer Nat King Cole in 1957.

Carter also wrote the two creepy 'Josey Wales' novels, the first of which, *Gone to Texas* (1973), was the basis for Clint Eastwood's much-praised film *The Outlaw Josey Wales* (1976). The American right habitually accuses Hollywood of being wildly liberal, yet in truth Eastwood's movie is just one of many that portray the South's 'cause' favourably. The irregulars whom Josey Wales was based on murdered black non-combatants with no qualms whatsoever.

Not in so many words

"Let them eat cake." Supposedly spoken by Marie Antoinette giving voice to aristocratic contempt for peasant suffering just before the 1789 French Revolution, these words actually come from Rousseau's *Confessions* (1782) and refers to an earlier aristocrat. In both French versions the "cake" is in fact "brioche".

The defenders of the Alamo died for slavery

The Texan defenders of the Alamo against Santa Anna's Mexican army in 1836 have never been universally admired, and reservations were expressed long before the emergence of politically correct academe. The Texan rebels fought and died for 'freedom', and for Texan independence from Mexico, but the right to keep slaves was fundamental to their cause, a fundamentalism that raised eyebrows in the Northern US States at the time, and now ensures that modern Texans must celebrate their founding fathers with some tact. The declaration of independence was approved by the Texan leaders on 2 March 1836, with a constitution approved on 17 March. Meanwhile, the Alamo had fallen to General Santa Anna's forces on 6 March, and the mood of the Texans was uncompromising. The Texan constitution denied citizenship to blacks and their descendants, prohibited the entry into Texas of free blacks and placed severe obstacles in the way of emancipation: the Texas Congress would not 'have the power to emancipate slaves: nor shall any slaveholder be able to emancipate his or her slaves without the consent of Congress.'

Texas was to be a hardline slave state, and it would be difficult to find any Alamo defenders who disagreed with that view. The Texans were mostly what Americans call the Scotch-Irish, ie Ulster Scots: Lowland Scots who had been 'planted' in Ulster in the 17th century, then came over to America in the 18th century – over a hundred thousand of them – bringing their ancestral memories of sieges, feuds and sudden bloody actions. They hated Catholics, they despised the English and they saw blacks as slaves and the Native Americans and Mexicans as distinctly inferior beings. Several of the Texan leaders were slave traders, including Jim Bowie, a man whose body was scarred with old stab and bullet wounds. Bowie's home county of Edgefield in South Carolina was an extremely violent place, settled by people whose ancestors had fought and feuded for centuries in the strife-torn Anglo-Scottish borderlands.

It is commonly said that men such as Bowie cannot be judged by modern standards, but historical empathy can surely only be stretched so far. At least Bowie was a genuine hard case. His fellow defender Davy Crockett has a massively undeserved heroic reputation. As Roberts and Olson say in their book on the Alamo, *A Line in the Sand* (2001), the term 'celebrity' came into use around 1850, when, with men such as Crockett becoming famous 'for being famous', it was much needed. Crockett's was the first celebrity death.

Popular myth gets at least one thing right about the Alamo: 'El Deguello', that ancient haunting song of no quarter, was indeed played outside the Alamo's walls as a promise of no mercy to the defenders, a promise given and kept as it had been by Spanish armies since the Moorish wars. One who was spared was William Travis's slave Joe, who was given his freedom by Santa Anna. The general pointed out to a presumably relieved and more than grateful Joe that Mexico had abolished slavery; a touching scene that somehow does not make it into the Hollywood versions of the battle.

The Wild West was not that wild

Parts of what we call the Wild West, during the canonical period of about 1860-90, were undoubtedly violent places, but the violence has been much exaggerated. To take a famous example, the Lincoln County War in New Mexico (*see **Director's cuts are not the*** *definitive version*) resulted in the deaths of perhaps 20 men from the murder of English rancher John Tunstall (who seems to have been a nice man) in 1877 to the death of his protégé Billy the Kid in 1881 – a rate of four to five killings a year. The Kid was a migrant from New York City, where the murder rate in areas such as the Bowery was a good bit higher than Lincoln County. New York was possibly not much worse than other American cities (though much worse than British ones), and the murder rate actually seems to have gone down from the 1850s onwards; in the 1850s there were officially about 30 murders annually (but the true murder rate in the slums was very likely a good deal higher). Lincoln County was on the whole more peaceful and less prone to ethnic tensions – and had better air quality.

According to just about every western we have ever seen, towns such as Dodge City and Abilene were littered with bodies. In fact, as the historian Richard Shenkman points out, Dodge's worst year for murders was 1878, when there were just five killings; Tombstone's worst year also saw five murders; Deadwood's worst, four. There is no recorded instance of a shoot-out anywhere at 'high noon', and the most famous showdown of them all, the OK Corral gunfight at Tombstone in 1881 which left three men dead, was not much more than a squalid settling of accounts among pimps and hoodlums – several of the victims were probably unarmed when shot.

Even the main Indian fighting was done 'off centre' from the west. Earlier conflict between whites and Native Americans in the east had been very fierce – King Philip's War of 1675-6 was particularly brutal, as was the so-called 'Northwest Indian War' of 1785-95 in which a Miami-Shawnee confederation inflicted more damage on the whites than the Lakota and Cheyenne combined ever managed.

The wildest and worst places for murders were not in the Not-really-so-wild-after-all West, nor in the cities, but in the old South, in states such as South Carolina, Georgia and Mississippi, where a slaveholder mentality that defined humans as property combined with a view of 'honour' that sanctioned violent retribution as normal created settlements where life could be remarkably cheap. The Sheperdson-Grangerford feud in *The Adventures of Huckleberry Finn* (1885) is not just Twain's coy way of introducing a Romeo and Juliet theme into his strange and often brutal novel; it is a fair account of the everyday bloody feuding of the time and place, as is the tarring and feathering in the book and the casual murder of a local drunk by a local killer. The high plains were a lot safer, and possibly still are.

Mounties wore red jackets to be seen by Native Americans

This statement is still regarded as unbelievable by many Americans, yet is perfectly true. The Northwest Mounted Police (they became 'Royal' in 1904) was formed as a corps of 300 men in 1873 to police Canada's frontier areas – in practice this meant patrolling the border with the USA, which is where bandits and 'wild' Native Americans would tend to be found.

The uniform from the first was closely modelled on that of Britain's redcoat army. The tunic was a smart and a very scarlet Norfolk jacket. The scarlet was to tie the new force into the traditions of the British Army, so that, as the official history says, 'the North-West Mounted Police would be readily identifiable with the reputation of their British predecessors (rather than the Americans in blue uniform) thereby gaining the confidence and respect of the First Nations'.

The red jackets were vital on the frontier for Native Americans, who would know they were safe in Canada ('the grandmother's country') when they saw a man in horseback in scarlet uniform. Canada was, however, perhaps not quite as welcoming as some Native Americans would wish. When Sitting Bull led his Hunkpapa people into Canada in November 1876 after the Lakota victory over Custer at the Battle of the Little Big Horn (*see Oral history cannot give you the whole picture*), a Major Walsh with just 26 men warned Sitting Bull that Canada was not to be used as a base for raids into the USA. The British, however, were prepared to give sanctuary to the Lakota, but not to feed them, nor were they willing to make the Lakota British citizens. This was despite the medals Sitting Bull produced which he said (quite plausibly) had been presented to his grandfather for Lakota help against the Americans during the Revolution. The Lakota drifted back and surrendered. Sitting Bull later gave something back to the British when he visited Canada with Buffalo Bill's show in 1885, handing out money to the children who followed him everywhere.

Apaches sometimes scalped

Of all North American Indians, Apaches have historically had the worst press: early novels and movies tended to show the Apache as ruthless killers and torturers so, as a corrective, modern studies emphasize the courage and spirit of Apache men and women, their long struggle against white imperialism, the manipulation of their tribal relations by Mexicans etc., and their renowned disdain for scalping. The point about scalps seems moot: if taken prisoner, it was what was done to one's body while still alive that would give cause for concern, not the shearing of your corpse. In fact, some Apaches did actually scalp but very rarely; scalping seems to have been an almost taboo ritual for some bands, for unclear cultural reasons. However, as was once observed, the finer points of cultural relativism would have been lost on travellers passing through or near Apacheria, that part of the American Southwest under Apache domination.

American popular culture, when featuring Apaches, often employed the bad injun/good injun pairing: in 1950s westerns, Cochise would do the noble speeches, while Geronimo would mutter darkly at the fork-tongued white man (though Cochise's torture and murder of white captives was well documented). In the 1960s this would change and the bad injuns became the good injuns, while the former good injuns became Native American Uncle Toms. That loose cannon of a movie *Ulzana's Raid* (1972) was much criticized for its violence and for portraying Apache tortures, but it is both a fine film and historically accurate. The real Ulzana (also called Jolsanny) broke out with 10 warriors in 1885 and murdered at least 38 people, 4 of them Apache children, and travelled a total of 1,200 miles. Geronimo was also raiding at the time in Arizona and Mexico, killing Mexicans for preference, but Americans also. His band had perhaps as few as 35 warriors at its peak, against which Washington sent a quarter of its army, some 5,000 men.

Apache culture was tough: feuds were commonplace and adulterous women had their noses cut off. James Kaywaykla, who was taken by Victorio's warrior band as a small child, said 'until I was ten years old I did not know that people died except by violence'. Kaywaykla died in 1963, and recorded that he saw 'hundreds' killed, but no one scalped.

Geronimo's final living warrior, Jason Betzinez, died in 1959, after publishing his remarkable autobiography that year, a landmark of elision in its absence of detail of constant killing. One of the odd things about Betzinez's book is the seemingly limitless gullibility of the Apaches, invariably falling for the Mexican trick of luring them in with a promise of alcohol and then massacring them when drunk. Apaches were notorious drunks and binged regularly on their own tiswin and white men's booze. They must have seen the danger in the Mexican offers, but the desire for the oblivion of alcohol was just too strong. It is a common belief that reservation life in itself drove Native Americans to drink, but – while this is obviously a delicate subject – it seems clear that some tribes such as the Apache had long-running problems with binge-drinking within their cultures, and other tribes didn't. Drink killed Geronimo in the end – he died from pneumonia in 1909 at the age of about 79, after drunkenly falling (either off a, quite literal, wagon or his own horse) and lying out all night.

The largest scalphunter band in Mexico was led by an Ulster Scot, James Kirker (1793-1853), a former prisoner of the Apaches whose band ('a fearful set to behold') possibly took around 500 Apache scalps for bounty in the 1830s. Arguably, the most dreaded scalphunter group in the Southwest (or anywhere) was a small, multiracial band led by a white man called Glanton at the end of the 1840s. They scalped Apaches for bounty and when Apaches were not about, were quite happy to scalp anybody.

The 7th Cavalry preferred clog dancing to baseball

The origins of baseball in America are much debated but remain obscure: like many 19th-century bat-and-ball games baseball very likely owes something to rounders, but cricket may be the strongest influence. Certainly, American cricket clubs encouraged it to spread, often fostering the sport as a sort of companion game at cricket grounds. By the 1870s, baseball had become patriotic, the 'national pastime'.

In the army some clung to older traditions. According to Elizabeth Custer, a close and loving observer of the 7th Cavalry, the heroes of the troopers were their clog dancers, 'the idols of the regiment'.

When camped at Big Creek in Kansas the men built 'a great room' to house their entertainments, 'dignified by the name of the Opera House'. The troopers took many devious measures to smuggle their clog outfits on active service. 'How they managed to carry their professional shoes and tights was always a mystery.'

Clog dancing could be pretty rough, closer in spirit to the world of Bill Tidy's cartoon strip *The Cloggies* than to any sanitized folk ceremony. The world centres for clog dancing were Lancashire and the Appalachian mountains, and it was a pastime for hard men. Elizabeth was realistic about the troopers who were her constant companions. They got drunk when they could and fought when they could, and not even her husband's authority could protect the legendary Wild Bill Hickok from death threats from the troopers when he was serving as the Hays City marshal.

Baseball seems to have been fostered by the army as a form of team building. In the 1880s at Fort Duchesne, in between battles with Utes and white desperados, the black troopers of the 9th Cavalry, the 'buffalo soldiers', played baseball (and also boxed) with white, mostly Irish, infantry. The matches were mostly amicable. Like clog dancing, the black troopers were quickly written out of western history. It was not until John Ford's *Sergeant Rutledge* (1960) that the buffalo soldiers got cinematic respect – the clog dancers are still waiting.

➤ *See also* **Oral history cannot give you the whole picture.**

Municipal parks are there to make you a better person

One of the most scabrous poems of any real quality in English is the Earl of Rochester's *A Ramble in St James's Park* (written c. 1672). The poem was and remains in some parts unquotable but is fine Restoration verse:

> There, by a most incestuous birth,
> Strange woods spring from the teeming earth,
> For they relate how heretofore,
> When ancient Pict began to whore...

St James's is London's oldest royal park: it began as a Tudor deer park and was finally opened to the public by Rochester's sometime friend Charles II. It was quite a pretty place, with neat lawns and picturesque tree-lined avenues, and Charles himself liked to come down and feed the ducks, mixing anonymously with his subjects. After dark, however, it became a dangerous place, haunted by footpads as well as debauched aristocrats.

It is unlikely that any royals or dukes thought that their parks, when open to the public, would actually make better people out of the visitors, but when the Americans began building municipal parks in the 19th century they did so in the full expectation that such places would improve the behaviour of the lower orders. Henry Ward Beecher sincerely believed that the divine beauty of such parks, located within city boundaries, would promote 'gentle thoughts and grateful silence' within the urban proletariat, and Frederick Law Olmsted, the architect who designed Central Park, while certainly envisioning enjoyment as part of the park's function, regarded it as having a much more serious purpose. Outlining in 1883 his plan for the Detroit Belle Isle park, Olmsted said that the value of a municipal park lay 'in its power to divert men from unwholesome, vicious, and destructive methods and habits of seeking recreation', and in its power to persuade the poor 'to educate themselves'. Olmsted resigned in high dudgeon when the Detroit city fathers started demanding amusements.

On both sides of the Pond it was expected that visitors to parks, in the imperfect present, would observe appropriate decorum and respect social hierarchy. This could not be legally imposed, of course, so parks such as the Derby arboretum (built by a local industrialist in 1840, and regarded as England's first public park) charged admission on selected days, thus restricting admission to those who could afford to pay. This ruled out the respectable poor (or 'scruff') but paradoxically let in the wealthier class of swindlers and prostitutes.

Henry Ford did cars in green with a red stripe

Henry Ford's most famous sayings are that 'history is bunk', and that 'a customer can have a car of any colour he wants, so long as it is black'. Although apocryphal, the remark about car production does seem to sum up his production-line philosophy (admired by Stalin and other dictators), but the evidence of the cars themselves does not quite match the quote.

Not in so many words

"Me Tarzan, you Jane." This famous misquotation derives from the meeting between Tarzan and Jane Parker in *Tarzan and the Ape Man* (1932). The encounter is nothing like as succinct as the 'quote' suggests and involves a lot of pointing and prodding and tedious repetiton of "Me" and "No" and "You" before Tarzan – at last – gets the point.

The first Model T was designed (not by Ford himself) in 1907 and the first models were not black. For the first few years they could – depending on body style – be red or grey, or even a fetching shade of green with a red stripe. The first standard paint was apparently 'Brewster Green' in 1910, a dark green, which was followed by a dark blue and then in 1913 a clever engineer suggested that black paint might dry faster, and for a dozen or so years Ford made its cars black. The company went back to colour choice in the mid-1920s, apparently as a result of increased competition, particularly from General Motors. By then, the Model T was a very outdated car, much behind the competition in technological terms, never mind colour.

There is a lot to dislike about Henry Ford: he was a vicious anti-Semite, a racist more generally and he used strike-breakers and the police against his workers (four striking workers were killed in 1932). But in some respects he was an astonishingly progressive employer. In 1919, Ford employed over 40,000 workers, of whom more than 9,000 were disabled, a rate that few if any large modern employers can match. He also gave jobs to women and believed that released convicts should be given a fresh chance at employment. And he paid well: five dollars a day in the early 20th century was a very good wage for a manual worker.

Prohibition was not a total failure

A nationwide 'prohibition' – a ban on the manufacture and sale of alcohol – was introduced into the USA in January 1920, and was repealed in December 1933. In the popular mind, prohibition was a total failure and made a mockery of the law. Even President Harding kept illegal liquor in the White House. The USA, it is said, was a laughing stock and the 18th Amendment banning booze had to be repealed.

In fact, repeal did not apply to all the states and Oklahoma, for example, did not legalize alcohol until 1948. Mississippi was the last hold-out, legalizing the alcohol trade as late as 1966 (bringing to an end an almost 60-year ban in the state). Lots of American citizens continue to live in 'dry' counties, practically all in the South.

Prohibition was introduced after a long campaign by Christian, temperance and women's organizations, acquiring greater impetus after the founding of the Anti-Saloon League in 1893. It has been suggested that the main target of the Anti-Saloon League was the growth of an Irish organized vote centring on urban saloons, and this in all likelihood was a factor that appealed to Republicans, but the rise in the 1890s and early 20th centuries of saloons is fairly re-markable. In many urban areas, mainly in the north-east, it is claimed that there was a ratio of 1 saloon to about 200 (or fewer) Americans. This seems improbable, but it is certainly the case that alcohol con-sumption was fast becoming a massive problem. Saloons competed vigorously for business, often becoming local centres for gambling and prostitution.

Prohibition certainly led to the consolidation of power by criminal gangs, gangs that often worked hand in glove with compliant au-thorities. Yet for all that, prohibition actually brought about much good. American consumption of alcohol declined sharply in the 1920s before rising slightly towards the end of the prohibition era. Tens of thousands of working-class men just lost the habit of drink-ing, and money was spent on children's food instead of drink. Many poorer children lived because of prohibition.

The American Civil Rights movement began with black servicemen stationed in Britain

Not long after American troops arrived in Britain during WWII, Osbert Lancaster drew a cartoon of a queue at a bus stop. The queue is a representative snapshot of British life, and includes that much-loved peer the Earl of Littlehampton and a black GI. The GI has his hands in his pockets and a fag in his mouth. Not an idealized portrait for sure, but not a racist one either, and therè is no question that he is entitled to his place in the queue. If the GI had been queuing in the US Southern states, his place would not be before white people. This attitude survived until the early 1960s, when it was fully expected that a black pregnant woman would stand on a bus, while white men sat – a situation that would have Northern whites averting their eyes and visiting Britons gibbering with fury.

When Lancaster drew the cartoon, blacks were still being lynched in the American South, and there was a good market for photographs and postcards of such lynchings (the US Mail only refused officially to deliver such cards in 1908). Amazingly, it was not until 2000 that this aspect of the *acceptability* of white brutality against blacks began to achieve recognition in the USA, with an exhibition of photocards (going up to 1960) being held in New York. The images are exceptionally disturbing, and the stories behind such lynchings are beyond belief: one man was hanged (with his dog) for not raising his hat to a white; Laura Nelson was hanged for trying to protect her 14-year-old child from a white mob (her child hangs beside her from a bridge). The photocards are not just from the backwoods, but are from cities such as Dallas, and the whites openly present their happy faces to the camera; they even bring their children, who smile and wave.

Throughout the 20th century there was a gradual increase of blacks (and whites) who were not prepared to tolerate segregation and persecution, but the major impetus for civil rights undoubtedly came from black servicemen stationed in England during WWII. British attitudes were hardly perfect: but the American army was so taken aback by the friendliness of the English towards blacks, that they made a training film for GIs (featuring Dan Duryea) advising them not to get upset when they saw blacks being invited into white houses. Several US army censors – see Stephen Ambrose's *Band of Brothers* (1992) – regarded black soldiers' frequent expressions of surprise and joy in letters home at their treatment in England as having deep implications for American society. They were right.

President Kennedy was not a doughnut

The myth here is so persuasive that like so many of its kind you feel it must be true: when President Kennedy made his emotional speech to Berliners in 1963, a speech designed to express solidarity with the people of Berlin in the face of the Communist threat, and used the phrase, 'Ich bin ein Berliner', the Berlin audience laughed out loud, a 'Berliner' being a word commonly used to refer to a type of doughnut; it is also generally insisted that you can hear the laughter of the Berlin crowd following Kennedy's words.

The kernel – or rather jam – of truth here is that Germany does indeed have doughnuts that are, in some places, called 'Berliners'; but not in Berlin. No Berliner would have had a sudden picture of Kennedy as a doughnut. Further, the film has been studied many times and there is no laughter from the Berlin audience – not a snigger – at Kennedy's remark. There was laughter from the audience shortly afterwards – after the translator had repeated his German words, Kennedy said 'I appreciate my interpreter translating my German', which got an appreciative laugh. But as has been pointed out, Berliners would be as likely to hear Kennedy saying 'I am a doughnut', as New Yorkers would be to hear 'I am a magazine', if a visiting politician said 'I am a New Yorker'.

The doughnut story is a product of its day, 1980s America, and its tenacity is possibly due to the gradual evaporation of the great Kennedy myth itself. It is difficult to imagine now how popular Kennedy was in the 60s and early 70s. Idealization of him reached its highest point in Irish homes all over the world, where saint-like portraits of Kennedy would hang in proximity to pictures of the Sacred Heart, with no hint of blasphemy. Kennedy's reputation has simply collapsed since the late 70s, with every aspect of his life being questioned, most notably his constant womanizing. It seems possible that, as time goes on, and as his reputation sinks further, that he will be mainly remembered as the source for the corrupt Mayor Quimby in *The Simpsons* – watch out for his 'Berliner' references…

President Kennedy did not ruin the hat industry

The notion that John F Kennedy ruined the hat industry by refusing to wear a hat for his presidential inauguration in 1961 became so widespread that someone wrote a book to disprove it: *Hatless Jack* (2005), by Neil Steinberg. In fact, as Steinberg points out, Kennedy did wear a hat to his inauguration, a black silk topper. Two years later, as Philip Larkin was to declare, the world changed for ever between the 'end of the Chatterley ban and the Beatles' first LP', and Kennedy's topper was unquestionably a madly archaic symbol by 1963, which is why many people forget JFK wore one. It just didn't match his contemporary image.

In any case, hats had been in decline since at least the 1920s. John Betjeman's poem on the death of King George V in 1936 identifies a key moment, when the young Edward lands to claim his throne: a man of the Jazz Age, modern and informal ('a young man lands hatless from the air'), watched by an older generation conscious of the past fading away.

Not wearing a hat in public was, until about the mid-1930s, a challenge to the social order, and a gesture that could earn the rebuke of total strangers. Hats were seen as serving useful social functions: the lower orders could doff them while meeting their betters, and gentlemen could show their manners by taking them off while being introduced to ladies. Not taking your hat off indoors was seen as highly rude and is still seen as an insult in traditional societies – in an episode of *The Sopranos*, Tony insists that a diner in a restaurant removes his baseball cap (the Mafia still seem keen on old-fashioned manners).

Until the early 20th century, doctors would quite seriously say that wearing a hat could prevent baldness, and would insist that white men going to the tropics should wear pith helmets – not because head covering under a hot sun is perfectly sensible for everyone in a hot climate, but because white men's brains were supposedly bigger and their skulls proportionally thinner than those of the rest of humanity.

➤ *See also* **President Kennedy was not a doughnut.**

The Gov'nor is not loved by all in Birmingham

One of Neil Young's most low-key, and certainly more preachy songs, is 'Southern Man', a dirge-like critique of whites in the American South and their appalling attitude to blacks. This worthy song annoyed the white Southern band, Lynyrd Skynyrd, who responded with 'Sweet Home Alabama', a rousingly self-confident lyrical defence of 'Southern Man'.

'Sweet Home Alabama' says that in Birmingham 'they love the Gov'nor', and also has a reference to not being bothered about Watergate. The Watergate reference is presumably intended to suggest that liberal concerns are not those of real Americans, and the 'Gov'nor' is clearly George Wallace, elected Governor of Alabama four times: 1962, 1970, 1974 and 1982; his wife, Lurleen, filled in for him in 1966 (she died in 1968). The reference is not fully explicit, but it has been suggested by some that the 'Gov'nor' is loved because of his last term, when, after becoming a born-again Christian, he abandoned his segregationist past and worked for black rights. Wallace changed, and the South also changed, and everyone was happy. The trouble with this rosy picture of reconciliation, one much promoted in Alabama for obvious reasons, is that not many blacks buy it (and the song was released in 1974 when Wallace was still unreconstructed). Unlike his horrible speechwriter Carter (*see **Little Tree was no Cherokee***), Wallace seems to have initially been a liberal on race who choose the bad when the good was not working for him.

Wallace had a 'good war', serving in the USAAF on missions over Japan; on his return to the USA, he worked as a lawyer and was elected to the Alabama state legislature. He was perceived as a liberal, and his actions were those of a liberal. Black defendants sought him out to be their lawyer, the NAACP saw him as an ally, and indeed endorsed him in elections. The turning point came in 1958, when a racist – with the open support of the KKK – defeated him in a Democratic primary election. Wallace notoriously vowed 'I'll never be outniggered again'. Later, after being 'born again', he would claim that the more extreme views he expressed were those of his speechwriters and not his own opinions, but blacks were not often convinced. He would say, for example, that he regretted saying Carter's words 'Segregation now! Segregation tomorrow! Segregation forever!', but no one noticed this lack of enthusiasm at the time.

As for Lynyrd Skynyrd, difficult though it is to refrain from cheering a song that celebrates poor whites in the face of middle-class disdain, Neil Young is the one in the right. Lynyrd Skynyrd would probably have done better to leave Wallace out of it.

Not in so many words

"Mirror mirror on the wall, who is the fairest of them all?" The Disney version of the evil queen's words in *Snow White* is actually "Magic mirror on the wall, who is the fairest of them all?" The classic 1898 translation of the Grimm fairy tale is also a bit different: "Mirror, mirror upon the wall, Who is the fairest of all?"

No peace activists spat at homecoming Vietnam veterans

This is an enduring legend that stems from the muddying of fact with fiction so endemic with the Vietnam War. The image of homecoming soldiers being spat upon by 'peaceniks' (to use a contemporary slur) is a disturbing one, even for such a divisive and unpopular conflict as Vietnam, but no one has so far identified any cases of it actually happening in real life. The myth has been thoroughly examined by the academic and Vietnam veteran Jerry Lembcke in his book *The Spitting Image: Myth, Memory and the Legacy of Vietnam* (2000). Lembcke points out that peace activists made a point of being friendly with veterans; people were indeed spat on, but the people doing the spitting were supporters of the war, not its opponents; indeed, the only vets who were spat on were members of Vietnam Veterans Against the War (Lembcke himself was a member of the latter group).

It is entirely possible, as Lembcke suggests, that the myth originated within the Nixon administration as a smear to discredit those against the war; and of course the smear has been a useful one for post-Nixon US governments engaged in debatable conflicts.

Another potent story about the Vietnam conflict is that the suicide and crime rate among veterans of the war is very high. A book called

Stolen Valor: How the Vietnam Generation Was Robbed of Its Heroes (1998) by B G Burkett challenges these and other generally accepted notions about Vietnam veterans. Burkett in turn has been accused of not giving due weight to the horrors of the war, but he undoubtedly has at least one strong point to make, that an awful lot of people falsely claim to have served in Vietnam. Their experiences derive from movies and from documentaries. In some cases this is a conscious deception, as an invented war service record may play well in court as a justification for criminal behaviour ('it was the war, man') but in a remarkable number of cases it seems to be an authentically held, if delusional, belief.

Curiously, in Australia it is the *children* of Vietnam vets who display a suicide rate three times higher than the average.

Tartan Day has little to do with Scotland

The sort of Scottish 'heritage' lauded in America has long been problematic for many Scots, and Scottish influence in US history has often been seen as malign by commentators. Mark Twain blamed Sir Walter Scott for the American Civil War, pointing out that plantation owners had come to believe, from reading too many Scott novels, that they were descended from Highland chiefs, and were noble beings whose rule of black 'children' was a benign part of nature (some even christened their sons and daughters after Scott characters).

The planter view was nonsense, of course; the descendants of the Highland upper classes, whether Whig or Jacobite, mostly all fled colonial America to Canada or Britain when the Revolution took place. But the fantasy remained, and is best illustrated by the scene in D W Griffith's silent masterpiece, *The Birth of a Nation* (1915), when Highland ancestry and culture is specifically invoked at the founding of the Ku Klux Klan. 'Here I raise the ancient symbol of an unconquered race of men, the fiery cross of old Scotland's hills . . . I quench its flames in the sweetest blood that ever stained the sands of Time!' The Klan makes much of its Scottish 'heritage' still. In this view, Scottish heritage is a white man's cult, and a part of Protestant culture also, unlike the longest-running 'Celtic' festival in America, the urban Catholic festival of St Patrick's Day.

'Tartan Day' was established in 1998 by Senator Trent Lott. Lott's questionable past on matters of race has never been that obscure, but that his old attitudes were still alive became clear in 2002 when he celebrated the 100th birthday of Strom Thurmond (the last American politician, incidentally, to receive the votes of Confederate veterans), and proclaimed that America should have voted for Thurmond (and presumably his segregationist policies) when he ran for president as a third-party candidate in 1948. George W Bush, whose own position on race has been clear and positive, quickly condemned Lott, who was Senate Majority Leader at the time.

The Tartan Day website (www.tartanday.com) is a hoot (perhaps 'hoots'), but does have its uses: where else could one discover that Prestwick in Ayrshire is twinned with Vandalia, Ohio?

American sports fans are not peaceable and non-violent

Americans see British football ('soccer') fans as incorrigibly violent. Even the better class of American TV shows such as *Buffy the Vampire Slayer* and *Frasier* have portrayed the Brit as more concerned with having a riot than watching a game. The final *Frasier* episode gave us the scary spectacle of Richard E. Grant and Robbie Coltrane as English soccer hooligans (with Coltrane's remarkable northern accent perhaps the most unnerving thing of all).

The Brits have long recognized the problem of course. Once you get problems of definition of bad behaviour out of the way – rugby fans are merely 'boisterous', but football fans are 'yobs' – there is no arguing with the fact that you would prefer to meet the rugby fans in the street, rather than the football ones. And the rise in hospital admission figures after, say, Rangers v. Celtic games cannot be denied.

Yet, as the journalist Steven Wells has said, violence among American sports fans is a major problem – it's just not a recognized problem. If Liverpool supporters forced a disabled Chelsea supporter to take off his supporters' top and then destroyed it, the incident would make national headlines; in the USA such incidents (this one happened at a Dallas Cowboys against Philadelphia Eagles match) are increasing. Travelling sports fans in the USA tend not to be attacked because they travel without identifying marks – the risks of being assaulted are just too great.

The problem is not just one of violent fans. Professional American basketball, hockey, baseball and American football players behave in ways that would be completely unacceptable in Europe. Eric Cantona's stupid kung fu kick against a fan is still seen in Britain as a high-water mark for bad professional behaviour, but in 2004 one of the Texas Rangers threw a chair at rival fans, breaking a woman's nose, just one of several incidents involving players throwing objects at fans. The *Christian Science Monitor*, here as so often one of the most daring American media sources, has pointed to the rise of instances of extreme violence, and even murder: in Florida, a youth baseball coach broke an umpire's jaw, and in Massachusetts the father of one young hockey player beat a coach to death during a match. Intimidation of match officials by fans and players is a growing phenomenon at every level of major sport in the USA and far outstrips anything that happens in Britain. Yet Americans of all political hues still believe that the British are the ones with the problem.

Colin Powell's career path is not highly inspirational for black Americans

Tony Blair admires Colin Powell, the former US Secretary of State (2001-05). Colin Powell may or may not admire Tony Blair, but he doesn't think much of Britain. He is fond of observing that in the US he rose to the rank of general, but in Britain he would only have made sergeant.

Observations such as this belong in the 'Only in America' category, whereby the successful American uses his or her rise to demonstrate the superiority of American society over all others. When the rest of the world finds this attitude either unbelievable or comic, this outrages some Americans; but in truth there are many Americans who also find such an attitude bizarre.

Does Powell have a point? The first thing to say is that British forces had black military leaders long before the USA did – a former slave commanded a Royal Navy frigate in the late 18th century, and Britain had at least one black officer as long ago as WWI; secondly, black soldiers of Powell's father's generation found living in Britain inspirational (*see **The American Civil Rights movement began with black servicemen stationed in Britain***); thirdly, Colin Powell is not

US black in origin: his parents came from Jamaica before his birth.

The woeful lack of success among African-Americans in the USA is compounded by the fact that a high proportion of successful blacks turn out to be either British citizens or the children of British citizens, such as Powell. There are various explanations as to why this should be so, but the most convincing is that the children of British West Indians come from a culture in which they are encouraged to succeed, and believe they can succeed. Colin Powell was brought up in the Bronx, where most black children fail, but where West Indian children do at least as well as other minorities. Failure is not written into their script.

As the bright son of aspirational parents, Powell was always going to do well, but his rise to high rank probably owed at least as much to his appreciation of the value of being a 'team player' as it did to active combat. Powell's first tour of duty in Vietnam was as an adviser to Vietnamese troops burning villages and crops to deprive Vietcong guerrillas of their support network. He later returned as a staff officer in the Americal Division, whose troops carried out the 16 March 1968 My Lai massacre of some 350 Vietnamese civilians, mostly women, children (and babies) and the elderly. Powell states in his autobiography that he was unaware of this massacre until some time after it happened (he joined the division in July 1968). Later that year Powell was given the job of investigating a complaint of routine brutality towards Vietnamese civilians which a divisional soldier had sent to the Commanding Officer of all US forces in Vietnam, General Abrams. Powell investigated the complaint by asking the man's superior officer if there was anything to the charges, and unsurprisingly received the answer that they were groundless. Powell was thus able to conclude in his report that 'relations between Americal soldiers and the Vietnamese people are excellent'.

(The helicopter crew who intervened and protected at least some of the civilians at My Lai were finally honoured by the US Army in 1998. Their names are Hugh Thompson and Lawrence Colburn; their crew chief, Glenn Andreotta, was killed later in the war – their names should be remembered.)

Writers, Language and Writing

The *Rubaiyat* may not be by Omar Khayyam

Not a great deal of it, anyway, and just possibly none at all. Much of what is said about Omar Khayyam (1048-1123) is highly contentious, but some things are fairly well accepted by the majority of scholars. Born in the Silk Road town of Nishapur, Iran (where he is also buried under a fine tomb), Khayyam (the name means 'tentmaker' in Farsi) was known principally as a mathematician and astronomer in his own time. It is confidently asserted by many that he was a Sufi, or was influenced by Sufism, but this is debated. He was an important mathematician, but statements about him beyond this point take off into speculation, and there are now many Omars: the secular, scientific one, the hedonistic poet, the devout Muslim serving God through his studies, the Persian patriot or the disseminator of Arabist culture. Some scholars say he may not have been known to his contemporaries as a poet in Farsi, and the Arabic verses attributed to him are quite pious in nature – unlike the speculative, agnostic quatrains of the *Rubaiyat*. Others say he was well known as a sceptic, indeed an atheist, with one Arab theologian describing his verses as 'snakes in the body of the holy law'.

The attribution of poems such as the *Rubaiyat* quatrains to Omar began in the decades following his death, when Shia clerics in the Middle East began restricting speculative thought. It is entirely possible that the name of Omar, as a venerated scholar, was a useful peg on which to hang sceptical thoughts. Over 1,000 quatrains have been attributed to Omar from the large body of heterodox medieval Persian verse, and this is probably how he has gradually acquired his reputation as a tipsy scholar musing on life, love and death, no doubt over some Persian version of Turkish Delight, and in the company of a maiden or young man in silk.

The *Rubaiyat* is best known in the English-speaking world from Edward Fitzgerald's translation of 1859. As has long been clear, Fitzgerald's work is a 'version' rather than a translation, and is more about Darwinism and Victorian doubts than anything to do with early medieval Persia. Indeed, the historian Robert Irwin has engagingly suggested that the Fitzgerald poem can be seen as 'a Norfolk eclogue inflected by loneliness and by the "Blue Devils" of melancholy' – not just a poem rooted in Victorian doubt, but an East Anglian hymn of despair comparable in modern times, says Irwin, to W G Sebald's *The Rings of Saturn* (1995).

Fitzgerald's sad lyric voice has made Omar a permanent part of English life: A S Byatt compared Fitzgerald's translation to the beating of the human heart: 'The iambic pentameter Fitzgerald used is the rhythm of our passing lives themselves.' We know, of course, that our passing lives can bear but little resemblance to the flowery world of the *Rubaiyat*, but we can feel profound for a while, thanks to Fitzgerald's magic and the original Persian poets, whoever they were.

The *Arabian Nights* were Persian

Debatable though cultural generalizations may be (*see* **Saladin was not an Arab**), it is safe to say that the *Arabian Nights* are not originally Arabian, but Persian. Arab culture has, however, certainly contributed to the tales. The original source is a Persian book called *Hazar Afsaneh* ('A Thousand Tales'), a collection of Indian-influenced tales emanating from Persia, which was translated into Arabic as early as the 9th, and possibly even 8th century. The oldest surviving written versions of the work are said to be a single page from the 10th century, and a partial 13th-century text from Syria.

The Persian work also provides the framing narrative of the whole, the story of a caliph who kills each wife the morning after the wedding, a custom brought to an end by the clever daughter (Shirazad or Scheherazade) of a vizier (the original characters have Persian, not Arab names). Later on the originals would be adapted and traditional tales from Baghdad and Egypt were added, thus 'Arabizing' the work to some extent.

The relationship of the stories to Arab and Persian and indeed western culture has become quite complex. Fictional narratives were often regarded as suspect in classical Islam, as being essentially deceitful (poetry was largely excepted). Indeed, the *Arabian Nights* has often been banned in Arab countries as both deceitful and immoral. Copies of an unexpurgated edition of the book were confiscated in Egypt as recently as 1985 as the work constituted 'a threat to the country's moral fabric'.

The strongest Arab element in the work seems to consist of the stories linked to the great caliph of Baghdad, Haroun al-Rashid, who ruled AD 786-809. The Sinbad story is doubtless Arab, but seems not to have formed any part of the *Arabian Nights* until a Frenchman, Antoine Galland, published a translation in 1701. He also included (and may even have invented or 'improved') the Aladdin stories and some Turkish tales. The western part in the collation of the tales into modern Arabic form is fairly significant. The 19th-century so-called 'Calcutta Texts' were designed to be a 'stimulating' (though cleaned-up) entry into Arabic for a growing British audience. It also has to be remembered that the tales clearly have their origin in ancient oral stories and efforts to pin them down too definitively to one culture or another are probably unwise. Tales, like trading, have linked the Mediterranean world for thousands of years and the desire for a precise origin is probably of more interest to Arab and Iranian nationalists than to the lovers of the work itself.

William Shakespeare the actor wrote Shakespeare's plays and poems

The theory that someone other than Shakespeare wrote Shakespeare's plays emerged in the mid-19th century as a response to a problem that was vexing many people: Shakespeare's works were increasingly seen as the greatest product of the human mind, so how could the author be a mere grammar-school boy from Warwickshire?

The answer was supplied in 1857 by an American, Delia Bacon, who argued that the author could only be a man of great intellect and profound knowledge, a man steeped in ancient and modern learning, speaking many languages and a statesman to boot. Indeed, the only possible candidate had to be her namesake (but no relation) Sir Francis Bacon. This theory (quickly dubbed the 'Baconian Heresy') led to the founding of the Baconian Society in 1886. Bacon had obviously hidden the evidence of his authorship in the plays, but cryptography (an interest of Bacon's) could find the answer. For example, the longest word in the plays, 'honorificabilitudinitatibus' (from *Love's Labour's Lost*), unscrambles to *Hi ludi F Baconis nati tuiti orbi*, which (in F E Halliday's translation) is Latin for 'These plays, F. Bacon's offspring, are preserved for the world'.

Cryptographers can have great fun with Shakespeare and Bacon. It can be shown, for example, that Bacon also wrote much of Elizabethan drama and (despite his death in 1626) the works of Alexander Pope (born in 1688). Various aristocrats have also been nominated for the honour of penning Shakespeare's works. It was either the Earl of Rutland or of Derby, and one Thomas Looney 'proved' it was the Earl of Oxford. Less noble candidates have included Christopher Marlowe (whose murder in 1593 was clearly faked so he could continue to write).

As is evident, a lot of the supposed 'controversy' about Shakespeare authorship was and remains principally a matter of simple snobbery combined with ignorance of how writers work. As Anthony Burgess pointed out, writers don't actually know everything they write about: something copied from a racing newsletter does not make you an expert on horses in real life, and writers appear from every background; Shakespeare's very learned contemporary Ben Jonson was a bricklayer (Shakespeare himself was the son of a glover).

A queasy aspect of all this nonsense is that it seems never enough to 'prove' that the actor Shakespeare was not the creator of the plays; he has to be insulted as well. He was a 'peasant', an 'ignoramus', a shadowy man held in contempt by all. In fact, Shakespeare was an active, indeed highly popular, member of London's theatrical community. The popularity is attested to by Hemmings and Condell, the actor friends who put together the First Folio of 1623, by the quarrelsome Jonson ('I loved the man'), by the printer Henry Chettle who (very unusually) apologized publicly for printing criticism of Shakespeare, and many others. It is often said that we know little of Shakespeare, but this is far from the truth; few writers of any age or in any land have been so generously praised by their contemporaries and peers.

There are only two portraits of Shakespeare with any claim to authenticity, by virtue of their status as being accepted by those who knew and loved him: the Droeshout engraving used as a frontispiece to the First Folio, and the family-commissioned Janssen bust in Stratford Church. Both are a bit unsatisfactory: the Droeshout portrait has been compared to that of a provincial lawyer, while the family bust shows someone who (in modern dress) might be a rather dim golf club secretary. More romantically inclined forgeries and doubtful (if hopeful) attributions abound, the best being the so-called 'Chandos' portrait, which the Victorians loathed because it looked 'foreign' (the swarthy complexion, and that earring!), but which looks much more pleasing to modern eyes.

Jane Austen knew her sailors and soldiers

Captain Benwick in Jane Austen's *Persuasion* is seen by most modern readers as something of a wimp. He mourns for his dead fiancée, and occasionally has a quiet weep. He is also perhaps a bit too fond of poetry. As Anne Elliot says to him: 'It was the misfortune of poetry, to be seldom safely enjoyed by those who enjoyed it completely; and that the strong feelings which alone could estimate it truly, were the very feelings which ought to taste it but sparingly.' Later on, of course, he falls in love with and marries Louisa Musgrave, who fell so romantically off the Lyme Regis pier.

Yet none of Austen's contemporaries would make the mistake of underestimating Benwick, who is first lieutenant of the frigate *Laconia*. The Royal Navy's frigates at this time were highly complex and deadly fighting machines, with brave and intelligent crews. Benwick is many things, and one of them is a killer of men, though that does not stop him also being a romantic who has over-indulged in the poems of Scott and Byron.

As always, Jane Austen is drawing from life. She prefers to write about Royal Navy men (her own much-loved brothers rose to become admirals) but there were romantics such as Benwick all over the place in Regency England.

The day after the siege and capture of Badajoz by Wellington's forces in 1812, a young Spanish lady asked British officers for protection from marauding British troops. The storming of Badajoz had been a bloody business. Wellington had been compelled to take the city by force, and cities taken by force were unsafe places for anyone in the immediate aftermath; rape and murder continued for two days before Wellington erected a gallows for his own men and stopped the terror.

The young woman had a 14-year-old sister, and the two were taken in and protected. Within a few more days the girl, Juana Maria de los Dolores de León, was married to young Harry Smith who had fallen in love with her. Smith became one of the British Army's most notable soldiers, in an era brimming over with remarkable soldiers. He was present at the burning of Washington (which he found a bit much after Wellington's relatively restrained warfare), at Waterloo (he was brigade-major at 28), and he had a long and devoted marriage to Juana Maria. In his own words, she had 'a sense of honour no knight ever exceeded in the most romantic days of chivalry, an understanding superior to her years, a masculine mind with a force of character no consideration could turn from her own just sense of rectitude, and all encased in a frame of Nature's fairest and most delicate moulding, the figure of an angel', etc., etc. They would spend almost 50 devoted years together, with Juana outliving her husband by 12 years.

Sir Harry (as he became) was later made governor of the Cape Colony, and the town of Ladysmith in South Africa is named after Juana.

Not in so many words

"Tomorrow to fresh fields, and pastures new." The last line of Milton's *Lycidas* is often given this added bit of alliteration, but the original has fresh "woods" not fields.

Jane Austen was not an apologist for the slave trade

The worst film ever made of a Jane Austen novel – indeed arguably the worst film ever made of a classic English novel – is Patricia Rozema's *Mansfield Park* (1999). The major problem with the film is not so much the explicit sex, the cavalier transfer of lines from one character to another, nor the ahistorical acting; it is entirely possible that Jane Austen herself would have been completely unfazed by such a treatment. It is unlikely, however, that she would have been pleased by the reduction of Sir Thomas Bertram to a pantomime villain and implied sexual abuser of children (this is probably the worst acting performance of Harold Pinter's career), and without question she would have been dismayed by the film's implicit message that she herself was unaware of the horrors of the slave trade, and of the West Indian foundation of the Bertram fortune.

This way of looking at *Mansfield Park* stems from Edward Said's analysis of the novel in *Culture and Imperialism* (1993). Said insists that any 'reading' (as critics are wont to say) of the novel must 'foreground' (as critics are also wont to say) the economic basis of the society from which it springs: 'Yes', says Said, 'Jane Austen belonged to a slave-owning society'. This view of literature as 'superstructure' is sometimes called a Marxist view, but Marx himself would certainly have rejected anything so simplistic as intellectually void.

Mansfield Park is perhaps Austen's deepest yet generally most unloved novel, and her quietist heroine Fanny Price is certainly her least-loved heroine, yet there is no doubting the seriousness of Austen's approach to moral issues in the novel. It would have been perfectly clear to Austen's contemporaries that Fanny and her beloved Edmund were evangelicals and as opposed to slavery as Jane Austen herself was (her two brothers, who became admirals, served in a Royal Navy that fought against slavers).

At one point in Rozema's movie, Edmund Bertram is made to say regarding the slave trade, 'We all live off the profits, Fanny, even you', a line that deserves some recognition for being, as the critic John Sutherland has said, perhaps the least likely line Austen would ever have written.

➤ *See also* **Jane Austen knew her sailors and soldiers.**

'Kangaroo' does not mean 'I don't know' in any Aboriginal language

The fable of Captain Cook and the kangaroo is an old and famous one, and it is entirely possible that there have been stories of this kind in circulation for as long as people have had encounters with radically different cultures. The story tells that Captain Cook landed his ship, the *Endeavour*, off north-east Australia in 1770, in what is now Cooktown, in order to make repairs. He spied a strange creature hopping along and, while pointing to it, asked a convenient Aborigine what the beast was called; the Aborigine replied 'I don't know', which in his language was 'kangaroo'.

Cook was not an unintelligent man (even if he was becoming increasingly irrational and aggressive). He was well aware of cultural misunderstandings (and could be said to have died of one, on Hawaii), so the misunderstanding between the curious Cook and the helpful native seems implausible. The truth is that while the repairs were being carried out, the great scientist Joseph Banks and other crew members were busy collecting specimens, and they were soon familiar with kangaroos. Cook recorded in his journal on 4 August 1770: 'The Kanguru are in the greatest number... we seldom went into the country without seeing some.' It is vastly unlikely that an initial misunderstanding could persist under these circumstances.

The ship's artist, Sydney Parkinson, made the first sketch, and Banks's description is the first by a scientist: 'an animal as large as a greyhound, of a mouse colour and very swift.' A member of the local tribe, the Guugu Yimithirr, passed on the name of the creature to the crew, 'gangaroo', which is their name for the grey kangaroo and does not mean 'I don't know' (there are reckoned to be about 200-300 living speakers of the language).

Admiral King is said to have recorded a different name in 1820, 'mee-nuah', and so the myth grew that the original English word 'kangaroo' really meant 'I don't know'. There were and are hundreds of languages in Australia, but linguists and historians are confident that 'kangaroo' is indeed from 'gangaroo' ('mee-nuah' or 'minha' seems to signify 'an edible animal').

Robert Burns wanted to be a slave overseer

The reputation of Robert Burns as a poet for all humanity seems secure. Many of his poems, such 'A Man's a Man for a' that' have become virtual world anthems, recited at Burns Suppers from Dallas to Dubai. His poem 'The Slave's Lament', written in 1792, was much recited at anti-slavery meetings in the 19th century. It begins:

> It was in sweet Senegal that my foes did me enthral
> For the lands of Virginia-ginia O;

> Torn from that lovely shore, and must never see it more,
> And alas! I am weary, weary O!

The poem is perhaps not one of Burns's finest lyrical works but it expresses very well the heartache and degradation inflicted upon millions by the slave trade. The odd thing is that a few years earlier Burns had considered becoming a slave overseer in the Scottish slave plantations in the West Indies. What prevented him going was the success in 1786 of his poems – the great 'Kilmarnock' edition, one of those remarkable volumes of poetry that comes along but rarely. According to Burns, he earned 'all expenses deducted near £20', a considerable sum. Burns describes his thoughts in anticipation of publication thus: 'twas a delicious idea that I would be called a clever fellow, even though it should never reach my ears a poor Negro-driver, or perhaps a victim to that inhospitable clime gone to the world of Spirits. . . I was pretty sure my poems would meet with some applause; but at the worst, the roar of the Atlantic would deafen the voice of Censure, and the novelty of west-Indian scenes make me forget Neglect.'

The syntax is ambiguous, but it does seem that in Burns's eyes, it is the driver who is 'poor', not the 'Negro'. The misery of life on the Scottish slave plantations was well known, indeed the anti-slavery movement had strong support in Scotland, so why Burns should have been so cavalier at the prospect of being a slave overseer remains obscure. Certainly, it is difficult to imagine another major poet in the English language of the late 18th century who would have reacted with anything but horror at the thought of being a slave overseer.

Frankenstein was neither a monster nor a baron

Since that masterpiece of the cinema, *Frankenstein* (1931), the monster (definitively played by Boris Karloff) has been commonly confused with his creator, Frankenstein. Such confusion is frequently corrected with a smug, 'Frankenstein is the baron, actually, not the monster', but such smugness is misplaced.

Mary Shelley's novel, *Frankenstein or the Modern Prometheus* (1818), is a Gothic novel but is also seen as the first true science-fiction novel. In nearly all of the films – a prominent exception is Kenneth

Branagh's *Mary Shelley's Frankenstein* (1994) – Victor Frankenstein has been given a title which he does not have in the original novel, where he is simply a young student, Dr Victor Frankenstein; he is not a baron at all. The films make him an aristocrat in order to give him an aura of a power that has become decadent. German barons are rarely good guys in the movies (the best they can be is misguided).

In the novel, Victor Frankenstein is not a bad man, he simply wants to create beings that are superior to humans. His 'creature' – also called 'fiend' or 'wretch' – has been made from bits of corpses and is far from mute (an early stage adaptation made him mute, and the cinema has largely followed this tradition). When he speaks, or reflects, he does so in the high tone of a querulous Regency gentleman: 'I thought of the occurrences of the day. What chiefly struck me was the gentle manners of these people, and I longed to join them, but dared not. I remembered too well the treatment I had suffered the night before from the barbarous villagers.'

The conflation of Frankenstein with his creation in the popular mind could be down to an unease many people feel about scientists (perhaps especially German ones), but it is perhaps mainly due to the splendid name itself: Frankenstein. If the creator had been called Schickelgruber or Gloop, the name would very likely not have migrated to the creation.

You can split infinitives if you wish

It is commonly believed that it is bad English to split an infinitive, but in fact it is perfectly allowable. A split infinitive is defined by Chambers as 'an infinitive with an adverb between "to" and the verb' and gives as an example the most famous split infinitive of them all, *Star Trek*'s 'to boldly go'. In fact, 'to boldly go' is a good example of a split infinitive that makes perfect sense, which is all one can ask of written communication. To say 'to go boldly' or 'boldly to go' does not convey quite the ringing import of the USS *Enterprise*'s mission statement.

The claim that split infinitives are 'wrong' probably derives from a false analogy with Latin; the Latin infinitive is a single unit and therefore, it is reasoned, an English infinitive should not be split. But few of the great writers of English have felt the need to apply such Latin rules to their writing.

The history of the split infinitive as a crime in written English has – with perhaps too much rigour – been identified with the rise of the British Empire. It was first identified as a policing matter for grammarians some time around the middle of the 19th century, but does not seem to have been actually named until the end of the imperial century. By the time the great language expert Henry Fowler published his *A Dictionary of Modern English Usage* in 1926, debate over split infinitive usage had become something of a bore for most users of the language. As Fowler says, the 'English-speaking world may be divided into those who neither know nor care what a split infinitive is, those who don't know, but care very much, those who know and approve, those who know and condemn, and those who know and distinguish'.

The easiest way for a copy editor to annoy a writer used to be to point out a split infinitive. This rarely happens now thanks to Raymond Chandler's famous response to his editor: 'when I split an infinitive, God damn it, I split it so it will stay split and when I interrupt the velvety smoothness of my more or less literate syntax with a few sudden words of bar-room vernacular, that is done with the eyes wide open and the mind relaxed and attentive'.

Lewis Carroll was not a paedophile

Lewis Carroll (the pen name of Charles Lutwidge Dodgson) was undoubtedly an unusual man. His best-known works, the *Alice* books, appeal (perhaps uniquely) to both children and scientists, containing as they do seemingly endless potential for analysis. Carroll was an Anglican clergyman and, in the Victorian manner, knowledgeable about many things, from mathematics and logic to natural history, and he was a highly gifted writer.

He was also a talented photographer, and would be remembered as such if he had never written a book. And the one thing everyone knows about Carroll is that he took photographs of naked (or seminaked) little girls and was (or was very likely) a paedophile (albeit a repressed one). The surmise that Carroll's interest in little girls was at the very least a bit unusual seems to have first surfaced in Langford Reed's 1932 biography, *The Life of Lewis Carroll,* and runs like a dark current through all subsequent Carroll study (Reed's assertion that Carroll lost interest in his young subjects when they reached puberty has been very influential). But one of the many odd things about Carroll (and his society) is that his interest in photographing little girls was perhaps not that odd: others did it, including two of the greatest photographers, Julia Margaret Cameron and Frank Meadow Sutcliffe. It seems obvious to us now that by the time Freud came along he was sorely needed, but Carroll and his contemporaries did not share our retrospective wisdom.

Carroll's biographer Karoline Leach addresses the issue in her study *In the Shadow of the Dreamchild* (1999). Leach makes a very good case for the argument that Carroll was really interested in adult women, and puts much of the blame onto Carroll's family for actually suppressing the evidence of this interest in women (in order, strange as it may seem, to protect his reputation). Leach makes the point that the photographs of women wearing bathing costume that Dodgson undoubtedly took have all, for whatever reason, disappeared.

Leach's conclusion that Carroll is innocent of having any paedophilic inclinations has been attacked, but the defence case seems pretty strong to most students of Carroll, and is now the established view.

Not in so many words

"Vee haf vays of making you talk..." is a line ready to be hissed by a pantomime Nazi torturer. The original version is in fact "We have ways to make men talk", said by Mohammed Khan, the wily villain of the 1935 Gary Cooper film *The Lives of a Bengal Lancer* – said, incidentally, to be Hitler's favourite film (though this has to be pure coincidence, surely...?).

Oscar Wilde was not photographed in drag

Richard Ellmann's biography *Oscar Wilde* was published in 1987 and became one of the bestselling literary biographies of the late 20th century. A large physical object, the book seemed the authoritative guide and is still an excellent read – but there are a few things wrong. Ellmann claims at the beginning of the book that Wilde caught syphilis when he was at Oxford and at the end that he died of it, yet there is no evidence at all for this. He died of cerebral meningitis and the doctors who treated him made no reference to syphilis being the cause.

Ellmann's leading error, however, is one of the finest clangers in any major biography. Wilde's play *Salome* was written in French and during rehearsals for performance in Britain in 1892 with Sarah Bernhardt in the title role it was refused a licence because it contained characters derived from the Bible. It was published in France in 1893, and the following year in English with illustrations by Aubrey Beardsley, the volume meeting with much abuse for its 'decadence'. Wilde was famously convicted of 'gross indecency' in 1895 and was still in prison when *Salome* was first performed at the Théâtre de L'Oeuvre in Paris. Only *The Daily Telegraph* deigned to note its appearance.

Ellmann's book reproduces a photograph supposedly of Oscar cross-dressed as his heroine and captioned as such, and many books, articles and media reports still exploit Ellmann's error for its sensationalist value. In fact, the person dressed as Salome in the photograph is actually the Hungarian soprano Alice Guszalewicz posing for a publicity photograph for a production of Richard Strauss's German-language opera version of the play in Cologne in 1906 (premiered in 1905, the opera is a far greater work than the play).

Guszalewicz, who, it is ungallantly said, was a Middle European built to last, did have a striking resemblance to the robustly built Oscar, but the jewellery and costume in the photograph are present in other photographs of her, thus removing any doubt.

Sherlock Holmes never wore a deerstalker

If asked what Sherlock Holmes looked like, we will all picture him in a deerstalker, yet, as *The Times Literary Supplement* diarist 'JC' has pointed out, he never actually wears one in any of the stories. In 'The Adventure of Silver Blaze', he has an ear-flapped travelling cap, but that's as far as it goes.

Nor does he smoke a fancy curved pipe (an image much used by tobacco firms): whenever it was the case that 'it is quite a three-pipe problem, and I beg that you won't speak to me for fifty minutes' ('The Red-Headed League') it was a common clay pipe he reached for, not an expensive meerschaum: 'Then he took down from the rack the old and oily clay pipe, which was to him as a counsellor, and, having it, he leaned back in his chair, with the thick blue cloud-wreaths spinning up from him, and a look of infinite languor in his face' ('A Case of Identity'). There is a briar pipe mentioned once in the stories, but the only pipes he actually seems to smoke are the common-as-muck clay ones. Nor is it anywhere mentioned in the stories that he wears a caped overcoat, though he occasionally throws on a cloak.

The classic image we all have of Holmes, with pipe, deerstalker and caped overcoat, is entirely the work of the original illustrator of the stories in *Strand* magazine, Sydney Paget. Paget apparently based the look of Holmes on his 'strikingly handsome' brother Walter.

Doyle's own image of Holmes was probably rather like his old tutor at Edinburgh University, Dr Joseph Bell, a brilliant diagnostician and certainly the main source for the great detective – 'You are yourself Sherlock Holmes, and well you know it', he told Bell, whom he described as a 'thin wiry, dark' man, 'with a high-nosed acute face, penetrating grey eyes, angular shoulders.' He 'would sit in his receiving room with a face like a Red Indian, and diagnose the people as they came in, before they even opened their mouths'.

Wendy existed before Peter Pan, Fiona did not exist before William Sharp

The playwright J M Barrie is generally credited with inventing the name 'Wendy' in *Peter Pan* but the name existed (albeit pretty scarcely) before then. Barrie created the character 'Wendy Darling' in his play *Peter Pan* (1904) and based the name on a child he knew, Margaret Henley (who died aged 6), who called Barrie 'my friendy', which seems to have come out as 'Fwendy' and/or 'Fwendy-Wendy'. Barrie frequently used his friends' children's names in his works (perhaps not an unmixed blessing for the children).

The name 'Wendy' was certainly very rare before *Peter Pan*, but there are recorded 19th-century examples, and it was used previously as either a girl's or a boy's name. It has also been suggested that it was used as a 'pet' form of Gwendolyn. In terms of popularity, however, Barrie might as well have invented the name. After a slow start, and various variant usages such as 'Wendi' and 'Wendie' (there have been two Chinese emperors called 'Wendi', but these are unlikely to have had much of an influence on British names), the name took off throughout the English-speaking world in the 1920s, reaching the height of its popularity in the 1970s.

The name 'Fiona' was, however, invented by Barrie's contemporary, the Scottish poet William Sharp. Sharp published poems and novels under his real name, but devised the first name 'Fiona' – from the Gaelic word 'fionn' meaning 'fair' – and adopted the pseudonym of 'Fiona Macleod' to write works in the newly fashionable 'Celtic Revival' mode, a genre that dealt in misty, often verbose recreations of an imagined British and Irish past that was as real as Barrie's Neverland. Sharp used to insist that Fiona was really a lady of his acquaintance (when told that Sharp dressed in female clothing while adopting the Fiona persona, the scholar W P Ker famously replied: 'Did he? The bitch!').

Oddly, both Sharp and Barrie, apart from being clever at inventing female names, wrote works that are generally regarded as having hidden depths. *Peter Pan*'s dark core has long been recognized, but the best of Sharp's lyrics – such as 'The Faery Song' – also have unsettling undercurrents, quite unlike the usual run of naff 'celtic' verse. Sharp's works were adapted into a libretto by the composer Rutland Boughton for his opera *The Immortal Hour*, which premièred at the first Glastonbury Festival (an 'English cultural revival' event, which lasted till 1926 – no relation to the later pop festival) 12 days after the outbreak of WWI. *The Immortal Hour*, still (and perhaps for ever) the only fairy opera composed by a communist, is, rather like Barrie and Sharp themselves, an odd yet brilliant production.

The Inuit do not have hundreds of words for snow

The notion that Eskimos (the Inuit) have a great many words for different kinds of snow is certainly something that seems as if it ought to be true. For example, the various folk of the British Isles (with Shetlanders perhaps in the lead) have lots of words and expressions for rain, from 'smir' (a light rain) to 'raining cats and dogs'.

The Inuit do not in fact have large numbers of words for snow; the story appears to derive from some kind of private joke within the discipline of anthropology. The myth probably begins with early 20th-century reports that the Inuit had several words for snow and has, as it were, snowballed from there. One list of reputed Eskimo terms for snow that circulates on the Internet is quite clearly a hoax: 'erolinyat: snow drifts containing the imprint of crazy lovers'.

The linguist Steve Pinker debunks the story in his authoritative work, *The Language Instinct* (1995), and says that at most there may be about a dozen Inuit words for snow, which would mean that there are a good deal fewer synonyms for snow in Inuit than there are for rain in English.

It is sometimes claimed that the now accepted term for the people we know as the 'Inuit' is a politically correct imposition on the 'Eskimo'. This is not so. The term 'Eskimo' itself may well be a derogatory term imposed on the Inuit by other Native American tribes, and possibly means 'eater of raw flesh', as Chambers has it. It is therefore wholly appropriate to use the term 'Inuit'. Another notable example of such an imposed name is 'Berber' ('barbarian'), which is what the Arab invaders called the North African people they conquered; the preferred term for people such as the footballer Zidane is 'Amazigh'.

Albert Camus did not play in goal for Algeria

This is an extraordinarily persistent and widespread myth: even the authoritative myth-busting TV show, *Qi* (hosted by Stephen Fry) repeats as truth the fable that Camus played in goal for the Algerian national football team. Camus did play in goal for the Algiers university team, Racing Universitaire d'Alger (RUA), but both his university and athletics career came to a halt in 1930, when he developed tuberculosis (from which he suffered for the rest of his life), after which he became a part-time student and scraped a living by tutoring and clerking.

At school he had wanted to become a professional footballer, and sporting, often specifically football, imagery occurs in Camus' works ('I learned… that a ball never arrives from the direction you expected it. That helped me in later life, especially in mainland France, where nobody plays straight'), particularly the so-called 'Algerian essays'. The quotation: 'All that I know most surely about morality and obligations, I owe to football' can be seen on t-shirts, but is not quite accurate. The academic Lincoln Allison has pointed out (as academics do) that this is a misquote – what Camus actually wrote in a 1957 article was: 'What I most surely know in the long run about morality and the obligations of men, I owe to sport, I learned it with RUA.'

The sporting metaphors and imagery have helped plonk Camus' name in media places traditionally foreign to philosophers of any kind, never mind French existentialists. Consequently, the goalkeeper myth is as likely to pop up in a tabloid as in a *Telegraph* article. But Camus does not need such illusory lustre. The collapse of the USSR and the subsequent eclipse of communism and its apologists has seen the rise of Camus' reputation in relation to that of his opponents, such as Sartre, who previously ruled the French philosophical roost.

History – Ancient and Medieval

The Egyptian pyramids were not built by slaves

Until very recently, it was accepted wisdom that the Egyptian pyramids at Giza were built using slave labour. This belief perhaps drew some strength from racist assumptions about 'primitive' construction projects relying upon a huge supply of largely disposable unskilled labour rather than skilled craftsmanship – but also, to be fair, from the guess that the pyramids are just so big that an army of slaves must have done the bulk of the work.

The Greek historian Herodotus visited the pyramids in the 5th century BC at a time when they were already more than 2,000 years old, and his estimate of the labour force involved was 100,000, a figure that has remained influential in guesstimates. There are about 100 pyramids in Egypt, but it is the three Giza pyramids that the word 'pyramid' conjures up, particularly the Great Pyramid of Khufu (or Cheops), which is the last surviving (and the oldest) of the seven wonders of the ancient world (and was the Old World's tallest building until the great cathedrals of the Middle Ages).

Ancient Egypt was a slave society and slaves very probably played some part in the construction of the Great Pyramid. But there is a growing consensus that the essential labour force was skilled – highly skilled – and not just a brute slave force. As for numbers, opinions vary but a figure of between 20,000 and 30,000 men working over a period of about 20 years seems to be about the mark.

There are lots of books and websites that argue for occult and/or alien involvement in pyramid construction, but the pyramids are demonstrably products of human ingenuity and skill: their creators had considerable strategic talent for handling long-term complex projects, but their work was also based upon centuries of building experience. They were not wizards or extraterrestrials, they were 'just' bloody good engineers.

➤ *See also* **Stonehenge was not built by Druids**

Otzi the Ice Man was not gay and is not cursed

The discovery of a well-preserved Neolithic body in the Alps in 1991 caused a wholly justified sensation. 'Otzi', as he was dubbed, had been in a glacier since around 3,300 BC, and was well-equipped for survival. With him he had tools for fire-making, dried fruit and sophisticated weapons including a yew bow; he was seen at first as a shepherd or hunter, or possibly a travelling trader. One journalist wrote a charming portrait of Otzi as an early European citizen, dying of hypothermia while making his way between peaceful communities.

Bizarre rumours about Otzi's madly hypothesized sexuality began almost immediately after his discovery. It was said he was homosexual; he had no penis; he was a castrated priest or shaman. His sperm was supposed to be still viable, and Austrian women allegedly made enquiries about how to be impregnated by him. This was all nonsense, of course, but was indicative of a widespread desire to make sense of the bizarre event of having someone transplanted (even as a corpse) into modernity from the Neolithic age.

Two years after his discovery someone finally noticed that Otzi had an arrowhead embedded in him. Suddenly we knew how Otzi had died. The arrow hit close to his lungs, shattered his shoulder blade and he would have bled to death within hours. DNA evidence from his arrowheads and dagger confirmed he had been in a deadly struggle with others (his arrows had DNA from two people).

In 2005, newspaper reports started mentioning a so-called 'Otzi curse', in the grand old tradition of 'mummy' curses – *see **Ancient Egyptian spells and curses didn't (and don't) work***. By the end of 2005 the BBC was reporting 'speculation' about a 'curse' and saying that seven people connected with the discovery of Otzi had died in 'unclear' circumstances. Quite why the BBC felt it should report such matters in such a manner is another and sadder story, but certainly there is no mystery about people dying (one of the 'mystery' deaths was of a climber caught in an 'unexpected' blizzard). And there are dozens if not hundreds of people connected with Otzi's discovery who are alive and well, and indeed in some cases litigating (there are various claimants to being the true finder of Otzi…).

Ancient Egyptian spells and curses didn't (and don't) work

Hollywood and popular fiction have a great time with Egyptian curses; the one thing everyone knows about Egyptian tombs is that they are best left undisturbed. Lord Carnarvon, for example, led the expedition that discovered Tutankhamun's tomb in Egypt's 'Valley of the Kings' in 1922, and the boy king's fabulous grave goods; unfortunately, there was an ancient curse associated with the tomb to discourage grave robbers, and Carnarvon died a few months after the tomb was finally opened in February 1923.

However, his co-excavator, Howard Carter, who did most of the work and opened the tomb personally, and was the first person (for millennia) to see Tutankhamun's sarcophagus, lived happily until 1939 dying at the age of 64 (and is buried in Putney). The majority of the expedition members, indeed, lived normal spans. There was no curse; in fact, robbers have been merrily plundering Egyptian tombs for thousands of years. In the Middle Ages, mummies were collected and shredded for their presumed medicinal value.

The first Hollywood movie about mummies to make a big impact was *The Mummy* (1932), with Boris Karloff wearing the bandages, but there had been several earlier silent films that dealt with the subject, a notable example being *Vengeance of Egypt* (1912), which involves Napoleon, a stolen ring and a mummy with glowing eyes. Such tales go back into the depths of the 19th century – they probably reflect some sort of colonial tension regarding the mysteries of the colonised in general, as well as that of Egypt in particular. The tales could be used for comic effect, as in Edgar Allan Poe's short story (of 1845), 'Some Words with a Mummy', but we are now habituated to mummies being menacing instead of a source of laughs (and doubtful remedies).

Stonehenge was not built by druids

Like the pyramids (*see **The Egyptian pyramids were not built by slaves***), Stonehenge and other megalithic monuments attract outlandish theorists. The legend that Stonehenge is some sort of 'Celtic' creation for druids was a favourite antiquarian explanation for the stone circle and remains so in some sections of

Not in so many words

"Yonda lies the castle of my fadda." This line is supposedly spoken (in broadest Bronx) by Tony Curtis in any of a number of historical films, most frequently cited being *The Black Shield of Falworth* (1954), but he never in fact said it.

the popular media, but has long been discredited. The so-called 'Celtic' peoples did not arrive in Britain until at least 600 BC, by which date Stonehenge was already very old: as the archaeologist Jacquetta Hawkes said, 'any connection with the Druids. . . is purely conjectural'.

Hawkes is also responsible for the much-quoted observation that: 'Every generation gets the Stonehenge it deserves – or desires'. William Blake saw it as a citadel of evil 'Natural Religion', a 'building of eternal death'; neopagans see the site as sacred to the old mother goddess; modern-day druids see it also as a place of natural harmony, a work of humans attuned to both the earth and the stars; occultists see it as a place of dark and light mysteries. In truth, we don't know much about what went on at Stonehenge. It seems now quite certain that this and other megalithic structures were designed and built with astronomical alignments in view. Stonehenge is actually a fairly late megalithic structure, and was probably constructed over an enormously long period of time, from before 3000 BC to around 1600 BC.

Clearly it was a ritual site of great importance and may well in fact have been used later by druids, though we know astonishingly little about the druid religion, which seems to have flourished around 200 BC (*see **Rod Stewart did not try to buy up every copy of the Wicker Man***). No songs, texts or legends survive. We know bits and pieces from Caesar, Pliny and others: we know that mistletoe was venerated, for example, but all of this information is filtered through outside eyes. So much of what is written about druidic ritual turns out to be conjecture. The people we call (or used to call) 'Celts' were headhunters and so it is claimed that heads may well have featured

111

in their rituals, but our knowledge is limited. The first modern Druid ceremony seems to have been in August 1905. As for visionary Stonehenges, *Spinal Tap* should have the last word with their song 'Stonehenge', described by Nigel as an 'anthem to my Druidic ancestors': 'Stonehenge/Tis a magic place where the moon doth rise/With a dragon's face/Stonehenge...'

It is unlikely that sacrificial victims were honoured to be chosen for sacrifice

When so-called 'bog bodies' such as Tollund Man began to be discovered in modern times, they presented historians and archaeologists with problems of interpretation. These bodies are found in peat bogs (which preserve them remarkably well) and range in date from 8000 BC to the early medieval period. The Romans had claimed that the Iron Age peoples they encountered in northern Europe used human sacrifice as both celebration and punishment, indeed Tacitus explicitly mentions transgressors being drowned in swamps. It is actually impossible to say if any of the bog bodies are either sacrifices or cases of common punishment, but it seems clear that in either case (if the distinction is indeed a meaningful one) that there were strong ritual elements to the killings (that they were mutilated before rather than after death also seems very likely), and certainly in the case of Irish finds, the victims were interred on tribal boundaries.

One of the significant things about the bog bodies is that their stomach contents have been preserved: we may never know why they were killed but we do know what they last ate. Some of the bodies contain the remains of hallucinogenic plant matter, and it has been claimed by some optimists that this is to ensure that the victim's last moments passed in a happy trance-like state, and the 'victims' may indeed have been willing participants in rituals designed for the wellbeing of the community. This is unlikely to be true. As the archaeologist Timothy Taylor says, the cocktails of drugs discovered, combined with the physical injuries, would have resulted in a very distressing death. It is extremely unlikely that Denmark's Grauballe Man or Tollund Man would have volunteered for their deaths.

Archaeologists are no different to ourselves; we all want our ancestors to have been as benign as we imagine ourselves to be. This can lead to groping for a cultural relativism that makes no sense. There have been attempts to portray sacrificial victims (in cultures which used human sacrifice) as being willing participants, but the relevant ruling elites, such as the central and south American cultures, seem not to have been too keen on volunteering themselves.

You cannot see the Great Wall of China from space

Whenever The Great Wall of China is mentioned it almost invariably comes with the comment that it is the only man-made object you can see from space. Exactly what is meant by 'from space' varies a lot, but if one defines it as the view from the space shuttle, at a height of about 130 miles, then you will need good binoculars to make out much below. The most notable man-made objects visible from the shuttle are perpetually illuminated cities at night. If one defines space as from the Moon, then you would need a powerful telescope indeed to see anything on Earth. The Great Wall is not much more than 25 feet wide at its widest: if a wall of that width were visible from space then there must be many other structures that are visible (the Millennium Dome in London is about 900 feet across, to take but one example). Not only is the Wall not visible from space, in some places it is in such poor condition it is not even visible from the Earth. No astronaut has seen it or photographed it.

The Wall has an extremely long history. Fortifications along some of the route may have begun as early as the 7th century BC but the first linking wall went up during the reign of the First Emperor, Qin Shi Huang, around 200 BC. There was much rebuilding during the 14th-17th centuries designed to protect the Empire from raids by Mongols and other nomads. Jorge Luis Borges, in his essay 'The Wall and the Books', sees the Wall as designed by the Emperor to enclose as much as to keep out, and connects the erection of the wall with the Emperor's burning of all books in China – both designed to erase the past and make the world anew (the Emperor's history was written by Confucian scholars who hated him for destroying the classics, and it seems clear he was not an agreeable man).

The condition of the Wall is poor and getting worse. Incredibly, in places it is still being used as a source for construction works. A common estimate has it that only around 20% of the Wall is in reasonable condition. The Gobi Desert is encroaching on it, and the line formed by the windblown desert sand has in fact been photographed from space. If desertification continues the sand line along the desert boundaries will become more visible, if not the Wall itself.

There is no real evidence for Boudicca's existence

Boudicca (formerly Boadicea) has long been a symbol of English pride and resistance. The Victorians especially adored her, drawing parallels with their own dear queen. She was the widow of an Iceni chieftain, and led a native revolt against the Romans around AD 60-61. The rebellion was immensely destructive. Major Roman settlements such as London, Colchester and St Albans were attacked and destroyed, as is demonstrated by the archaeological evidence, a sinister line of red clay that has been dubbed 'Boudicca's Destruction Horizon' – the sooty remains of the great burning of the Roman cities. Boudicca is thus one of the significant figures in British history.

Or she may not be, because she may never have existed. The main sources for the revolt are Tacitus (writing at least 30 years after the events) and Dio Cassius (about 100 years after). The Romans had a fascination with the wild tribes of northern Europe, the British in particular, and were not above lacing their accounts of the Celts with moral lessons for the Roman world. Tacitus had a special interest in Britain: his father-in-law Agricola was governor here, and he wrote Agricola's biography. When Tacitus quotes the British chieftain Calgacus as saying (in a pre-battle speech) of the Romans 'They make a desolation and call it peace', we simply don't know if Calgacus actually said any such thing. But it is very much the sort of thing a Roman moralist would say, and the consensus is that Tacitus made it up.

But did he make up people too? The problem for the sceptics is that Tacitus knew men who served at the time, so why not just report what they said; why invent a warrior queen?

Something was certainly going on around AD 60, but the extent and nature of any revolt is unknown, and even the spooky 'Boudicca Horizon' is perhaps not that conclusive: fires happen, and in any case not everything was burned, except in Colchester where the entire town was systematically razed. Colchester, a centre of Roman cultural influence, was perhaps the most obvious target for native vengeance, yet archaeologists find no evidence of a wholesale massacre – the town was possibly evacuated, yet perhaps also the whole period was simply one of an eruption of bloody traditional feuding, in which attitudes to the Romans would certainly have been a strong factor. And the main figure of the anti-Roman faction may or may not have been a woman called Boudicca, who may (as tradition has it) be buried under platform 8 at Kings Cross station (just a few feet from where Harry Potter catches the Hogwarts Express at platform 9 3/4).

In 2001 the Iron Age grave (c. 300 BC) of a woman buried with a chariot was found at Wetwang in Yorkshire, evidence at last that there were women riding about in chariots before the Romans came. The chariots were clearly light and fast, and we can at least be sure that if Boudicca rode one into battle (as Tacitus alleges) it did not have scythes or blades sticking out of the side.

Roman houses did not have a room called a vomitorium

Even those of who are not greatly knowledgeable about the domestic life of ancient Rome know that the Romans vomited up between courses so that they could eat more (yuck!). To do this they went into a room called a 'vomitorium' and would then return with empty stomachs to eat more larks' tongues and goose eggs in pastry.

Except they didn't. A 'vomitorium' in Roman times was not a room but an access passage, most famously in amphitheatres such as the Colosseum, and had nothing to do with food except as a metaphor: vomitoriums functioned as safety features, through which crowds were safely channelled or 'spewed' out at the end of a performance. In any case, it is physiologically quite difficult to eat food directly after you have regurgitated: your stomach doesn't like it any more than your aesthetic senses would. The way you feel about it just now, reading this (just imagine those honeyed dormice shooting out of your mouth…), is pretty much how most Romans would also have felt: disgusted. A small number of upper-class Romans did indeed practise induced vomiting but this practice, mentioned by Seneca and a few others, seems to have belonged in the realm of what we have learned to call the 'differently pleasured' (such practices still exist it seems).

As it happens, we have a description (albeit fictional) of a banquet that has always been held to be an accurate enough portrait of the nouveau riche Roman dining experience – Trimalchio's Feast in Petronius's *Satyricon* – and we can be sure that if induced vomiting was something that better-off Romans did, then there would have been some way in which social-climbing Trimalchio would have got it wrong. Trimalchio got the idea, for example, that farting while eating in company is perfectly acceptable (*see* **Public flatulence is not good manners in Arabian society**). At one point during the banquet, Trimalchio's boyfriend Croesus does get his puppy to eat bread and vomit it back up, but this seems to be just another example of the appalling crudeness of the household. Petronius was one of Nero's courtiers and a connoisseur of perversion, both a brilliant writer, and a terrible snob.

Masada is a myth

The American TV mini-series *Masada* was broadcast in the USA in 1981 and tells the story of the Jewish revolt against Rome in AD 72-73. The Jews move onto the rock plateau of Masada where they defy a besieging Roman army (led by Peter O'Toole at his noblest). The Romans eventually take the stronghold by building a ramp construction and the Jews, after an inspirational speech by their leader, commit suicide to deny the Romans a moral as well as an actual victory.

The mini-series undoubtedly represents at least one strand of thought about what happened at Masada. According to the Jewish historian Josephus, the defenders were Sicarii (the name means 'daggermen', and they were regarded as extreme Zealots), who had been expelled from Jerusalem after the destruction of the city by Roman forces. The Sicarii garrisoned the stronghold and raided against Romans and Jews alike. The Roman 10th legion took the stronghold in AD 73 and Josephus got the story of the speech and the mass suicide of over 900 rebels from two women who hid with their children in a cistern.

The Masada siege is regarded by many Israelis as a symbol of national identity, of heroic resistance against huge odds. As historian David Lowenthal puts it, visitors 'come to Masada today not for tangible evidence of the ancient legend but to experience a modern passion play of national rebirth'. The Israeli archaeologist Yigael Yadin addressed Israeli army recruits at the site thus: 'Four thousand years of your own history look down upon you.'

Yet the external evidence for the Josephus story is wholly lacking. There is no corroboration from any other texts and the archaeological evidence does not support the theory of a mass suicide. And it is Israeli scholars such as Nachman Ben-Yehuda who have been at the forefront of criticizing the story. As Ben-Yehuda says, the story is an early 20th-century 'mythical narrative', and he points out that the 'Masada myth was basically created by secular Jews from about 1925 to the early 1960s – and not by observant Jews. Observant Jews are not too excited about the Masada myth – not then and not now.'

❝

Not in so many words

"You can fool some of the people all of the time, and all of the people some of the time, but you cannot fool all of the people all of the time." This is one of the many quotations falsely attributed to Abraham Lincoln, and is also ascribed to Phineas Barnum, but there is no evidence either of them ever actually said it (Barnum, the circus entrepreneur, would doubtless have said it with more wistful regret than Lincoln...).

❞

There is no great mystery about Rome's Fall

In Mitchell Smith's scary novel about prison life, *Stone City* (1990), an educated prisoner is asked why Rome fell when it had been so powerful. The answer given is taxes: the taxes just weren't coming in any more, so the structure fell apart. Auden's poem 'The Fall of Rome' gives the usual suspects of imperial decay, decadence, military arrogance, the ennui of the administrators and distant movements of animals and peoples ('Silently and very fast'). All factors here are related, but it is the end of the flow of tax money from Auden's 'provincial towns' that does it for the Empire. An empire without revenue will have no order.

The Roman Empire was rather good at accommodating invaders, and indeed turning the invaders – such as the Goths – into defenders. This depended, however, on the incomers wanting to adopt Roman culture, and it does seem that Rome had lost its appeal to the increasingly undefended peoples of the periphery. If the Empire could not defend its own people, then perhaps the culture was not that impressive after all. The new invaders (such as the Huns) took over the settlements, the locals made their accommodation with them and more sources of imperial funds dried up.

The Roman Empire did not have to fall. The eastern part, centred on Constantinople, lasted until 1453. It is commonly supposed that Christianity brought a 'civilizing' effect to the empire in its dying days, but this – to say the least – is heatedly debated. Certainly the dark side of Roman culture did not end with Constantine's establishment of Christianity as the imperial religion in AD 324. The persecution of non-official religions intensified. Ancient pagan sites in Hellenic lands were sacked and their adherents massacred, and while gladiatorial games fell out of favour, the execution of criminals and heretics in the arenas continued (gladiators cost money to train, but it cost little to have a prisoner slaughtered).

The moral aspect of any imperial dream is impossible to measure, but has to be taken into account with Rome's fall. Cruelty is certainly a constant in human nature, and other cultures of the day killed humans and animals in rituals, but there is an air of madness about the Roman slaughter, butchery on an industrial scale that emptied vast areas of the empire of wild animals.

Significantly, the institution of the arena was not copied by the wild peoples on the frontier. Long before the acknowledged end, the fall of the last emperor in AD 476, there was really not much for outsiders to admire or be envious about.

The Great Library of Alexandria was not destroyed by the Arabs

The ancient library of Alexandria (it was also a shrine to the Muses) seems to have been greatly expanded during the reign of Ptolemy II in the 3rd century BC, and included not just Greek and Egyptian classics but writings from all over the known world, including India. The city fell to the Arabs in AD 642 during the Muslim conquest of Egypt by the forces of Omar Ibn al-Khattab. It was claimed by later commentators that the city was largely destroyed by the Arab forces, and that when scholars pleaded with Omar to spare the great library and its collection of rare and unique works, he replied that if the library contained information that agreed with what was in the Koran then it was superfluous, and if it contained information that contradicted what was in the Koran, then it contained blasphemy, so it should be burned. Omar's orders were carried out and the world's greatest (and irreplaceable) collection of classic texts went up in smoke.

This still current story is one of several versions of what happened to Alexandria's magnificent library, but it seems probable (much of what is stated as fact about the destruction turns out to be highly contentious) that the great library's contents had been substantially destroyed or dispersed long before the Muslim conquerors arrived. The Roman historian Livy is said to have claimed (the original account is lost) that much of the library's contents – over 400,000 texts – were destroyed in 48 BC during the civil war between Cleopatra (with Caesar's backing) and her brother Ptolemy XIV, though many scholars say the number is quite improbable. Plutarch, in his biography of Caesar, says that Caesar started a fire that burned down the library, and Plutarch (who died c. 120 AD) actually visited the city, which gives some weight to his assertion.

There were continual periods of ethnic, political and religious unrest in Alexandria in the centuries following Caesar, and the 18th-century deist historian Edward Gibbon (who certainly had an anti-Christian agenda) claimed that the library was sacked during the reign of Emperor Theodosius, who began a campaign against paganism in AD 391. Gibbon's (inevitably contested) thesis is that the library – which of course contained huge numbers of pagan texts

– was destroyed in that year by a Christian mob led by Theophilus, the Patriarch of Alexandria, and its contents were set alight on bonfires. It does seem (consensus is rare on this subject) that there was an attack on the Serapeum (the most prominent pagan temple) by Theophilus's mob and that its library – possibly containing some of the original great library – was destroyed.

In AD 415 the Neoplatonist philosopher Hypatia, whose status as a female teacher seems to have been as offensive to the Roman Empire's new rulers as her disbelief in the new religion, was torn apart by a Christian mob. Hypatia was the last prominent member of a long line of pagan intellectuals. When the Arabs came in 642, there could not have been much of the pagan heritage left for the latest monotheists to destroy. It is possible, as some scholars believe, that they indeed happily destroyed what was left, but that was very likely only a remnant of the greatest pagan library.

Your local reactionary is unlikely to be 'to the right of Genghis Khan'

The phrase 'to the right of Genghis Khan' is sometimes applied to any politician of strikingly right-wing views (Attila the Hun is similarly used as a benchmark), yet is highly inappropriate. Genghis Khan does not really fit into the spectrum model of politics, in which extreme right is far removed from extreme left.

Genghis Khan was born c. 1162 and died in 1227. As a boy, he was called Temujin, and he had a difficult childhood, succeeding his father as head of his feuding clan at the age of 13. He eventually united the Mongols, and then set out conquering other peoples. The scale of the killing involved in the conquests was enormous, though it seems impossible that a final agreed figure will be arrived at. A figure in the tens of millions seems likely. After his death, the Empire spread east and west. The destruction of Baghdad in 1258 – a tragedy for civilization – was accompanied by wholesale slaughter.

In modern Mongolia – where Genghis Khan is revered – the deaths are seen as regrettable, but perhaps dwelt on too much. The end he sought was a good one, it is said, and the Mongols boasted that under his rule a girl could walk unmolested from Persia to China with a bag of gold.

The truth is that Genghis Khan was a collectivist, one of the most thorough-going who has ever lived. The so-called 'Great Yasa' of Genghis Khan is a varied collection of his maxims and thoughts, a code of government. How much of the collection actually derives directly from him is not known, but the collectivist spirit is authentic enough. The whole purpose of the Mongol Empire was to spread and bring more and more subject peoples into the fold, and this growing empire needed a code to regulate it. Some of the surviving decrees seem bonkers, and perhaps originally had some symbolic meaning: for example, someone who chokes on food is to be put to death. But as with all collectivism, obedience is the key point.

One area where there was tolerance was religion. The majority of the Mongols were animists, but there were Christians, Muslims and Buddhists too; indeed, Christian services were held in Genghis's camp, and his grandson married a Nestorian Christian.

The phrase 'to the right of Genghis Khan' may in fact have been inspired by John Wayne's awful film *The Conqueror* (1956), in which he played the Khan in the manner of a Texan out to avenge the Alamo. The film includes this wonderful speech from the Khan, besotted with his love for Bortai (Susan Hayward): 'There are moments for wisdom and moments when I listen to my blood; my blood says, take this Tartar woman.'

The Bayeux Tapestry is not an infallible guide to King Harold's death

The image we all have of King Harold's death – hit with an arrow at the Battle of Hastings – may be correct, but the issue is still vigorously debated. The fatal arrow scene is supposedly depicted in the Bayeux Tapestry, with a warrior clutching at an arrow seemingly embedded in his right eye. The word 'Harold' above and surrounding the head has generally been taken to indicate the figure is the Anglo-Saxon king. The next 'scene' along shows a mounted warrior striking down a knight who falls to the ground in the company of a large two-handed English axe. The revisionist theory here is that it is this figure which is Harold.

Most authorities do stick to the traditional view that the figure pulling at the arrow is indeed Harold. It is the explanation that makes most sense, and also agrees with the near-contemporary observation of the poet Baudri of Bourgeuil, who said (around 1100) of the tapestry that 'a shaft pierces Harold with deadly doom'. It is claimed by some that this section of the tapestry was tampered with while being restored in the late 18th century and the figure may have been holding a spear and not an arrow, but there seems to be no evidence of tampering with the image from the stitching.

The fact that an eye wound could also be seen as a spiritual wound – the Normans were keen to portray Harold as a blasphemous oath-breaker (having failed to honour his oath recognizing William's claim to the English throne) – leads some to suspect that the figure is indeed Harold but that the arrow strike is symbolic. In this view, both the figure struck by the arrow and the figure struck by the knight could be Harold, but the latter's death is the real one, with the fallen axe representing England and the eye wound representing Harold's blasphemy, which has delivered his kingdom to William.

The Bayeux Tapestry is not, strictly speaking, a tapestry at all but an embroidery. Formerly a largely undisputed object, the more the tapestry is studied, the more controversial it becomes. Many of the formerly secure assumptions have become debatable. It was commissioned by Bishop Odo (who is depicted in the tapestry), undoubtedly to celebrate the conquest, but some observers see subversive messages in it. The English were famous for their embroidery in the 10th and 11th centuries, and it now seems very likely (if you are not French) that the tapestry is the work of English, and not French, women (in France it is known as Queen Matilda's Tapestry). It is huge: 231 feet long with possibly as much as 20 feet missing, and its survival is remarkable. At one point during the French Revolution it was used as a cover for a supply wagon but was fortuitously saved.

The Normans did not introduce 'feudalism' into England

As with the Bayeux Tapestry (*see **The Bayeux Tapestry is not an infallible guide to King Harold's death***), explanations of the origin of feudalism used to be simple: feudalism came in with the Normans, was a 'Bad Thing' and gradually we all grew out of it at some point towards the end of the Middle Ages. Marxist scholars in particular loved discussing feudalism, because they could write for ages about the (slowly) Rising Bourgeoisie, working its way through centuries of noble and peasant life like a very lazy yeast.

But nowadays scholars find feudalism increasingly difficult to explain in detail with much confidence, so burdened has the term become with qualifications. The *Chambers Dictionary* usefully defines feudalism as 'a system of social organization prevalent in western Europe in the Middle Ages, in which powerful land-owning lords granted degrees of privilege and protection to lesser subjects holding a range of positions within a rigid social hierarchy'.

Beyond this point, however, debates about feudalism are best left to specialist historians. The notion that the Normans introduced feudalism into England is often combined with the belief that the Norman Conquest was a catastrophe, a perception that seems in many ways valid. William was one of the most ruthless rulers ever known in these islands. He dealt with rebellion in the north by mass slaughter, and parcelled out England to supporters who then treated the land and its people as naked plunder. William the Conqueror was indeed a monster, an alien gangster, but he did not – it seems – bring in a new ready-made system of 'feudalism'.

The Normans did not tinker too much with the Anglo-Saxon administrative structure and very largely kept the old shire system. The ancient system of patronage intensified, with new overlords who spoke a different language – French was the language of parliament until nearly 300 years after the Conquest – but the relation of the Norman duchy itself to its French overlord shows how problematic the term 'feudalism' is. The Normans disregarded the French king when they could get away with it and probably expected the same to happen with what used to be called their 'vassals' (another increasingly disused term in medieval history). At the end of the summer, the crops had to be gathered in and the pigs slaughtered, and you needed a healthy peasantry, and markets and tradesmen to oil the wheels of commerce – neat social structures of duty and dependency came a poor second to these imperatives. Daft as it seems, the supposedly anachronistic 'anarcho-syndicalist commune' depicted in *Monty Python and the Holy Grail* (1975) very likely does reflect accurately at least some aspects of the way of life of medieval English peasants.

Saladin was not an Arab

The great 'Arab' leader Saladin was not an Arab at all, but a Kurd, although some Arab nationalists, embarrassed at a Kurd ruling Arabs, have described him rather peevishly as an Arab 'by inclination'. His father was governor of Baalbek, and from this Syrian base Saladin rose to power fighting for Egypt against the Christian kingdom of Jerusalem. The Egyptian army was largely Shi'ite, whereas Saladin was a Sunni with a Syrian army. He managed to establish Sunni power in Egypt and also declared independence from the Seljuk Turks. He established the Ayyubid Dynasty, which ruled Egypt, Syria and parts of Iraq for several centuries.

Despite his reputation as a great foe of the crusaders, Saladin's main aim at first was not to expel the Crusaders from the Middle East but to exploit the Crusader Kingdom as a buffer state against his Muslim enemies. He often lost in early encounters with the Crusaders, but when he turned on them in earnest he won decisively, expelling the Crusaders from much of their territory and recapturing Jerusalem in 1187 (after almost 90 years of Crusader occupation).

Saladin had something of a special relationship with Richard I of England, and many of the stories about this odd mutual affection (an affection felt mostly on Saladin's part possibly) are true, though they never in fact met (Sir Walter Scott made up the desert meeting). During one battle, Saladin sent Richard two horses when his horse was killed underneath him; he also sent him sherbet and fruit when he was poorly, and offered him his personal physician.

Saladin was greatly admired by his Christian contemporaries. He died with few possessions in 1193 at the age of about 54, having given his wealth away. When Dante wrote *The Divine Comedy*, he placed Muhammad in Hell but Saladin in Purgatory, with the great thinkers of the past: 'I saw Great Saladin, aloof and alone.'

Saladin's reputation even increased during the 18th-century Enlightenment, when intellectuals would often contrast the brutal, ignorant Christian west with dignified, tolerant Muslims such as Saladin, and Sir Walter Scott established him firmly in western popular culture as a wise and tolerant ruler faced with western desperados. This version of a tolerant Muslim culture is something of a debater's construct, but Saladin himself certainly seems to have been a better man and better ruler than his Christian contemporaries.

Droit de seigneur must have been an extremely rare (and rather dangerous) aristocratic perk

In one of the many historically inaccurate scenes in *Braveheart*, an invading English lord demands the right to have sex with a fair Scottish maiden on her wedding night. This practice, also called *jus primae noctis* (law of the first night), was supposed to be enshrined in feudal law and is certainly so in the popular imagination. However, it is in fact the medieval equivalent of an urban legend, and falls squarely under the 'Braveheart Rule' of Scottish history ('if you saw it in *Braveheart*, don't rely on it being true').

The function of this scene – apart from the slickly contrived sadism so typical of the movie – is to further establish the evil of the English ruling class; yet, oddly, one of the very few European accounts of this supposed practice refers to a Scottish king's decree that lords are entitled to the maidenheads of virgins living on their land. But this account is by the notorious Scottish fabulist Hector Boece, in his *Scotorum Historiae* (1527), and the king he refers to never existed.

Much of the previously accepted wisdom on medieval times has been revised in the late 20th century (*see **The Normans did not introduce 'feudalism' into England**), and *jus primae noctis* seems to have arisen as a misunderstanding of some prevailing legal customs whereby 'peasants' (and the definition of the term 'peasant' itself can be problematic) may have required their lord's permission to marry. The *Droit de Seigneur* of a local lord was rigorously applied in hunting terms, and also in terms of the local ruler's right to tax people within his (or her) land. The practice of rape (as one should call it) in this context is said to have occurred in a very few parts of medieval France, in connection with unpaid dues. However, even these few isolated cases may be a misunderstanding of highly localized customs. Certainly nothing like the scene in *Braveheart* ever happened. In the real worlds of medieval Scotland or England, any lord who practised *jus primae noctis* would likely have had his throat cut within weeks, and his overlord's response would doubtless have been 'hell mend him'.

Not in so many words

"You dirty rat!" This is the signature line for James Cagney impressionists. In fact, in the 1931 film *Blonde Crazy* he exclaims "that dirty, double-crossin' rat!" – close, but not quite right.

No one wore chastity belts in the Middle Ages

It has long been believed in popular culture that medieval lords locked their women up in metal chastity belts when they left their castle, usually on their way to fight in a Crusade. There have been many cartoons on the subject, if very little wit. The idea of metal chastity belts could of course only have occurred to someone with limited knowledge of female physiology. Such belts would have to have been made of iron, stainless steel not being available, and would have resulted in fairly major health and hygiene problems. The improbabilities increase: the wife of a medieval lord would herself have belonged to a noble family, and, while many beliefs about medieval chivalry and honour are highly debatable (*see* **The Normans did not introduce 'feudalism' into England**), it is extremely unlikely that the wife's family would or could have tolerated such an insult. Also, the lady of the manor (or castle) would have been expected to take over the running of the house – with a steward and other staff for help – and an iron girdle would have put a real block on necessary mobility.

There are references in medieval poems to chastity belts, but these are all thought to be metaphorical and reflect a desire on the part of both parties for fidelity. There is a reference to blacksmith-fashioned iron belts designed to make sexual intercourse impractical (with the blacksmith secretly keeping second keys) by a 16th-century French writer, Pierre de Bourdeilles, but this is fairly clearly an example of French 'wit' and is not intended to depict something that actually happened.

All known examples of supposed chastity belts are of 19th-century origin. Until quite recently even major museums, such as the British Museum, had iron chastity belts on display as genuine medieval objects, but all have gradually and quietly been slipped into deep storage. In the late 19th and early 20th centuries, several forms of 'chastity' belts were invented – mostly by Scots for some no doubt dark Calvinist reason, such as one Dr John Moodie – in order not to prevent sexual intercourse, but to prevent masturbation. These strange and terrible devices, in both female and male versions, are as appalling as they sound (web research is most definitely not advised), and can be found in medical catalogues as late as the 1930s. There is also a market in modern times for chastity belts, as there is for many Victorian fetishistic inventions.

➤ *See also **Droit de Seigneur must have been an extremely rare (and rather dangerous) aristocratic perk.***

The Declaration of Arbroath celebrates ethnic cleansing and genocide

The Declaration of Arbroath was drawn up in 1320 by the Scottish nobles and is seen as Scotland's declaration of independence. Indeed, it is claimed by some as a source document for the American Declaration of Independence, and a 'Tartan Day' in the USA is held each 6 April on the anniversary of the signing (*see **Tartan Day is not for the Scots***). The document was apparently drawn up by the Abbot of Arbroath from drafts by the Scottish lords and is one of three letters sent to Pope John XXII in Avignon (where the papacy was in exile from Rome), the other two being one from the bishops, and one from Robert the Bruce. At the time, relations between the papacy and Scotland were bad; Bruce had been excommunicated for murdering one of his rivals for the throne, the 'Red Comyn', and the whole nation had been placed under papal interdict – which effectively meant national excommunication.

The papal copy has not survived, but one kept in Scotland, decorated with pretty seals and ribbons from the earls and barons, is in Scotland's national archive. The document is seen as the first statement of Scottish independence, and is claimed to have wider implication in its emphasis on the contractual nature of monarchical rule with the people of Scotland (the 'people' here being represented by the lords). In fact, just 12 years before the Arbroath declaration, Edward II's Coronation Oath of 1308 made the English monarch swear his adherence to 'the rightful laws and the customs which the community of the realm shall determine'.

The Arbroath document could not have been much of a direct source for the American Declaration of Independence, as it was largely ignored until the 19th century. The two documents are most similar perhaps in regard to the self-proclaimed idealism and self-lessness of the signers (or sealers) of both documents – whether they were baron or slaveholder – but they are quite different in religious terms. The Scottish one proclaims that Christ sent Andrew to convert the Scots ('almost the first') because of the Scots' 'true nobility and merits'. The American declaration is explicitly not a Christian document and refers to 'Nature's God' (the signatories were deists mostly, not theists; as Jefferson said: 'I do not find in our particular superstition of Christianity one redeeming feature'). The Scottish declaration is startlingly blunt in its celebration of the right of conquest of the strong over the weak, boasting that the Scottish invaders drove the ancient Britons from their homeland and exterminated the Picts ('The Britons they first drove out, the Picts they utterly destroyed'). This does align the spirit of Arbroath, however, with the American Founding Fathers, who complained that the British government was stopping them from expanding into and seizing the lands of what the Declaration calls 'the merciless Indian Savages'. Indeed, the need for military expansion into Indian territory – an expansion the British did not want – is as central to the American War of Independence as the American desire to keep slavery (*see The US Founding Fathers were not too keen on freedom and democracy*).

The Hundred Years War did not last 100 years

It lasted longer. The Hundred Years War in fact went on for 116 years. The war, fought between England and France, is generally held to have begun in 1337 and limped to a bloody conclusion in 1453. It was actually a series of smaller wars and conflicts with intermissions. Its origins lie in the muddy world of claim and counter-claim among Norman and other French powers and the roots predate the Norman Conquest of 1066 (indeed go back to the 10th century).

The great prizes were the fertile lands of Normandy and other French provinces – land that produced wealth. France had the advantage of a much larger population (and the English had also of course the Scots at their northern border, eager to take advantage of any mishap). But the French had the huge disadvantage of having the war fought on French soil, as England gradually took control of the seas.

Over the long stretch of the war, updated versions of old weapons, such as the Welsh longbow, were used to devastating effect by the English, and new weapons such as effective artillery came into use, new strategies emerged and of course new players. By the time the grandchildren (and great-grandchildren) had finished the fight their ancestors had started, Europe had changed irrevocably. Estimates of the total killed vary. A figure of around 185,000 battlefield deaths has been suggested, but many non-combatants were also killed or died of war-induced famine. The population of France declined by about a third over the period, a loss of around 6 million people by one estimate (the outbreak of the Black Death, which ravaged Europe in 1348-50, was clearly responsible for much of this decline; 40% of the French population died, and the English death toll was probably comparable.)

One war that did last its designated span was the Thirty Years War (1618-48), which was fought mostly on German and central European ground and resulted in a terrible death toll: perhaps 7 million.

There was no William Tell

A nation's founding heroes are expected to have (usually improbably) high standards in their lives but as a bare requirement are usually expected to have actually existed. In Switzerland, William Tell is revered as the national hero, and those Swiss who point out that there is no real evidence for his existence have been denounced as traitors, with some of the denunciations taking on a really nasty flavour, especially those involving accusations of 'internationalism', a word that carries echoes of the old euphemism for Jews, 'cosmopolitan'.

Several versions of the William Tell story began appearing in the late 15th-century and were consolidated into one coherent version in the late 16th century. The story tells of events that are said to have happened at the beginning of the 14th century, when the Swiss cantons were under Austrian domination. In the canton of Uri, the evil Austrian Hermann Gessler (the very essence of Germanic oppressor for generations of British as well as Swiss children) forces the great crossbow marksman to shoot an apple off the top of his son's head, which Tell does. When Tell tells Gessler that he would have been next if the boy had been hit, Tell is arrested but escapes, and the subsequent rebellion leads to Switzerland's independence from Austria.

It is a fine story but, like many other such stories is almost certainly no more than that, as indeed was already suspected in the 17th century. Reaction by the Swiss to scepticism about this tall Tell tale has traditionally been fierce. In the 18th century a pamphlet arguing that the story was just a fable was publicly burned in Switzerland.

There are in fact several such tales found in Scandinavian and Saxon story-telling and beyond, and no serious historian believes that the tale reflects anything more than the desire of the Swiss for a founding myth.

History – Renaissance to 19th Century

No one laughed at Christopher Columbus

According to George and Ira Gershwin, "they all laughed at Christopher Columbus when he said the world was round". The notion that medieval people believed the earth was round stems from Washington Irving, whose *The Life and Voyages of Christopher Columbus* (1828) invented the story that Columbus set out on his 1492 voyage to prove that the earth was round, not flat. Columbus did in fact have to face some doubters, but they were questioning his estimates for the circumference of the earth. Many felt, quite rightly, that Japan had to be further to the west than Columbus thought. Luckily for Columbus, America was in the way (he thought the Cuban mountains were the Himalayas).

There had been flat-earthers in the past, notably the 3rd-century scholar Lactantius, but the idea that the earth is flat was always seen as a cranky view from at least the time of Periclean Athens. The curvature of the earth has always been evident to sailors, who can watch ships and landmarks rising up on the horizon. The earth is not, in fact, quite round, and is actually an oblate spheroid, but that's round enough for most people.

Columbus himself is now a controversial and bitterly contested figure. He is seen as a hero by many Americans, particularly by Italian-Americans (he was possibly born in Genoa) and by Spain, on whose behalf he 'discovered' America. It has also been argued that he was Portuguese, Catalan, Basque, or of Spanish-Jewish descent. There are two 'rival' statues of him in New York's Central Park, each funded separately by the Italian-American and Hispanic communities.

In an episode of *The Sopranos*, mobster and family man Tony Soprano says: 'In this house, Christopher Columbus is a hero. End of story.' Yet Native Americans can only regard Columbus as a hate figure, as the man who brought white conquest and exploitation to the Americas, and it has become increasingly difficult for unhyphenated Americans to celebrate Columbus as they formerly did. He used slaves for sex, began the Atlantic slave trade by exporting Native American slaves to Europe, and chopped the hands off slaves who failed to deliver impossible gold quotas, the victims being left to bleed to death as examples to the others. Whatever Columbus now signifies, it is certainly not laughter.

Sir Thomas More was not a tolerant man

Thanks to Robert Bolt's play *A Man for All Seasons* and the subsequent 1966 movie starring Paul Scofield, Thomas More has acquired something of a saintly reputation. He is of course a saint anyway in the eyes of the Roman Catholic church, who refer to him as St Thomas More, but to most people – whose knowledge of the man comes from dim remembrances of the movie – he was a great, principled man who stood up for toleration in the face of a bad, intolerant Robert Shaw, playing Henry VIII with gusto.

Henry VIII cannot be rehabilitated. He was a very fine musician and composer and a true intellectual; unfortunately, none of this was allowed to get in the way of his appetites. In dramatic terms, he makes a good contrast with the high-minded Thomas More, to the latter's advantage. But Thomas More himself can be contrasted – and not to his advantage – with William Tyndale, the Protestant priest and scholar who translated the Bible into English 1525-31. Tyndale is one of the forgotten masters of English prose: the King James Bible repeats much of his fine writing, and when it veers from it does so, usually, to no great improvement.

Tyndale's works prompted a response from More in 1529, and the two subsequently debated their positions – from a distance, of course, and in print, as More wanted to kill Tyndale for his views. The debate is a curious one. Several scholars have asserted that the debate is between a modern (Tyndale) and a medieval (More) mind, with Tyndale winning on all fronts (More's style is actually reminiscent not so much of medieval thinkers as of a Soviet apparatchik fuming against an absent dissident).

More's style is knockabout, scabrous and petty, while Tyndale refrains from abuse and argues to the point. More and his wretched monarch eventually got their man. English agents arranged for Tyndale to be burned at the stake in Belgium in 1536. More was not there to gloat, however, as he himself had been executed by Henry in 1535, for treason. He was beheaded of course, a much quicker death than Tyndale's, or the many other 'heretics' More pursued. In his role as Chancellor, More had 6 Protestants burned alive and around 40 others imprisoned.

Christian churches did not burn nine million witches

In the 1970s, feminists and wiccan groups would often claim that there had been a mass murder of 'wise' women in Europe during the early-modern period. Huge numbers were bandied about – hundreds of thousands, perhaps up to nine million. This mass persecution was seen as an assault on the old, matriarchal, nature-orientated, goddess-worshipping religion of Europe (a religion that had survived underground) by a misogynist male hegemony. Scholarly estimates for the number of killings during the 'European Witch Craze' of the 16th and 17th centuries (a real enough phenomenon) are now in the region of 40,000 to 50,000 executions, with around 100,000 trials (about 20-25% of the victims being men).

Two other major misconceptions about this period are that the churches were the leading persecutors, and that witches were always burnt. In fact, secular courts were often much more likely to convict than ecclesiastical ones, and witches were often hanged or drowned rather than burned.

The main period of witch persecution was roughly between 1550 and 1650 and the numbers and factors involved varied widely from country to country: Ireland is known to have executed 4 witches, Germany around 26,000. Over 90% of Iceland's executions were of male witches. In Spain, the Inquisition seems to have been mostly concerned with protecting those accused of witchcraft. England executed fewer than a thousand, with the so-called 'Witchfinder General' Matthew Hopkins accounting for around 200 of those at the end of the English Civil War. Scotland executed over 1,300.

Scotland is an interesting case. Cromwell's administrators in Scotland were taken aback at the prevalence of witch trials, and the last witch to be executed in Britain was the old and befuddled Janet Horne in 1727, in Dornoch; Janet was burned alive in a tar barrel. After the

UK Parliament passed the 1736 Witchcraft Act banning executions, the Church of Scotland protested that the Act of Union meant Scots could no longer execute witches. The witch persecution in Scotland was an almost entirely Lowland phenomenon: there were no executions in Catholic Highland areas.

Thanks to Arthur Miller, the early 1950s, when communists were 'seen' everywhere in American life, are often compared to 1692 Salem and the witch trials there. *The Crucible* (1953) is a fine play, but the parallel has the effect of reducing the complexity of what happened at Salem: one judge resigned rather than take part; another, Judge Sewall (also a noted opponent of slavery), formally apologized for the trials in 1697.

The killing of women as witches continues in some parts of modern Africa; it has been suggested that at least 300 women were killed as witches in South Africa in the period 1986-96.

Not in so many words

"Luke, I am your father." What Darth Vader actually says to Luke Skywalker in *The Empire Strikes Back* (1980) is "No, I am your father". In *Toy Story 2* (1999), after Buzz says "You killed my father", Zurg replies, "No Buzz, I am your father".

Sir Francis Drake was a pirate and privateer

Drake has long been one of England's great heroes, partly because of who he fought against. Spain was far and away the strongest country of the day, and England not much more than a peripheral power. Drake's raids on the Spanish treasure fleets put Elizabeth I in an awkward position. The wealth he brought to England was of immense significance, yet war with Philip II of Spain would be highly dangerous.

Philip's decision to invade England was in fact practically inevitable. The heretical queen and her support for rebels and pirates could not be tolerated. In July 1588, Spain's massive Armada swung slowly into the English Channel (the story that Drake was playing bowls at

Plymouth when the Armada arrived dates from 1624 and may actually be true). The English fleet under Admiral Howard – Drake was vice-admiral – engaged cautiously. The galleon *San Salvador* exploded and as the day wore on the English ships followed the Spanish up the Channel, Drake's orders being to lead with a stern lantern in the *Revenge* for the others to follow. Unfortunately, Drake saw the opportunity to take a prize: the *Rosario* was in trouble. Drake astonishingly disobeyed orders and abandoned his lead position (the lantern may never have been lit) and the *Rosario* and its treasure were in his hands. Later on, at Gravelines, it was Howard's turn to abandon his position for some private looting, and it was Drake who took the attack to the Spanish, driving them out into the 'Protestant Wind' that carried the great Armada into the North Sea.

For many of Drake's peers among the English captains, his reputation as the great Protestant hero was nonsense. He may have been legally a privateer licensed with letters of marque against the Spanish ships for most of his fighting life, but Frobisher and others would have agreed with the Spanish that Drake was a pirate through and through. His seizure of the *Rosario* endangered the English campaign, though Drake increased his country's wealth as well as his own (he kept maybe half of the 50,000 ducats captured, a huge sum).

Seven years after the defeat of the Armada, the Spanish took one of the pettiest revenges in history, when they attacked a defenceless Cornwall and burned Mousehole (the Spanish commander described the churches in Cornwall as 'mosques').

When Drake died in the Caribbean in 1596 there was great rejoicing in Spain at the death of the country's greatest enemy. They had reason to celebrate, but the damage was already done. Drake's attritional raids on Spanish shipping had badly weakened Spain, and ships assembled to combat Drake left treasure ships vulnerable to other English (and Dutch) attacks. Drake was not the great patriot the Victorians believed him to be, but though a pirate at heart, he damaged Spanish power irretrievably. He was doubtless patriot enough to be pleased about that.

There really was a Gunpowder Plot

Conspiracy theories are not just a modern phenomenon. The instinct to suspect and hopefully ferret out the 'Real Story' may be part of what makes us successful primates, ie we are wired to examine and distrust a cause and effect that is perhaps too apparent. In the case of the Gunpowder Plot of 1605, the temptation to make a case for the whole thing being just a conspiracy to justify state repression – particularly of Roman Catholics – has been especially strong. Certainly it has always suited some governments to portray a small part of their citizens as potentially subversive, in order to unite the bulk of the population around it.

Not many modern authorities would accept this view of the 'Gunpowder Plot', however. The Jacobean secret service was both efficient and ruthless, but as historian Ronald Hutton has said, the idea that the whole thing was a government plot 'now has the status of the theory that Bacon wrote Shakespeare's plays' (*see* **William Shakespeare the actor wrote Shakespeare's plays and poems**). As a 400th anniversary flurry of books in late 2005 demonstrated, the plot was the work of a group of educated and pious young men who believed that they were doing the work of God.

The Gunpowder Plot, had it succeeded, would have been one of the biggest man-made explosions in British history. Its intended consequence, the accession of James I's nine-year-old daughter to the throne (her brothers having perished in the explosion), would almost certainly never have happened. The real tragedy was that English Catholics were deeply patriotic and, despite the fact that the plot was revealed by a Catholic aristocrat, its main consequence was a long delay in Catholic emancipation.

The king himself interviewed Fawkes, who said at one point that his aim had been to blow the Scots back to Scotland, a comment suppressed by the government as there was much popular resentment in London at the many self-enriching Scots who had accompanied James to London when he succeeded to the throne in 1603.

Cromwell fought according to contemporary rules of war in Ireland

Cromwell's reputation in Ireland used to be certain: he was one of the greatest monsters who ever lived and committed one of the greatest war crimes in history, the sack of Drogheda.

The context in which the sieges of Drogheda and Wexford happened was one of civil war tearing both Britain and Ireland apart. When Cromwell landed in Ireland in 1649, the 1641 massacres of Protestant settlers by the Irish was still a fresh wound (the number of victims was exaggerated, but the generally accepted figure of 10-12,000 deaths is still a huge number).

Drogheda was a Royalist stronghold and a tough nut to crack – its governor Sir Arthur Aston said 'He who could take Drogheda could take hell' and assumed that Cromwell's army would be starved into submission. In fact, the local Irish happily sold food to the troops, and Cromwell hanged two of his men for stealing a hen (Cromwell had imposed strict orders against looting or any misbehaviour). Negotiations took place, but Aston refused to surrender (and threw his grandmother out for plotting against him) and the storming of the city took place, with, as was customary, no quarter being given to defenders (Sir Arthur was beaten to death with his wooden leg). Innocent people must have been killed. As author Antonia Fraser points out, it is difficult not to arm yourself when your town is being taken by force.

Were Cromwell's actions here (and at the taking of Wexford later) excessive? In the context of the Thirty Years War, which had just limped to a bloody conclusion after the ravaging of much of Europe, the answer is certainly no. There was no great outrage at the time, and Cromwell only began to be really reviled in Ireland in the mid-19th century. The end of the 20th century saw historians look again at what actually happened. The Irish historian Tom Reilly has been criticized for his revisionist study of Cromwell's campaign, but Reilly makes the point that the speed with which the administrations of both Drogheda and Wexford picked themselves up is solid evidence against the wholesale slaughter of locals.

A case in England which is comparable in circumstances if not in numbers took place at Basing House in Hampshire in 1645, where

Cromwell's troops killed around 100 of the defenders after refusal of surrender terms.

Comparison of the 'monster' Cromwell with the Royalist hero Alasdair MacColla is instructive. MacColla landed in Scotland in 1644, and threw his Irish troops into Montrose's Royalist campaign. While laying waste to the Campbell lands in Argyll, he committed the worst of his many war crimes at Laganmor, where he had prisoners and the glen's women and children herded into a barn and burned alive. Cromwell, as all biographers attest, was never quite at ease with the Irish campaign; MacColla could see children burned alive without a recorded qualm. Yet Cromwell is the one who gets the opprobrium.

The Ottoman Caliphate was not fundamentalist

Some Islamic fundamentalists like to make threatening noises about restoring the 'Caliphate'. Most westerners are unsure what the Caliphate was, but are quite certain it must have been a 'Bad Thing' if Muslim extremists want it back.

When people refer to the re-establishment of the 'Caliphate' they generally mean the Ottoman Caliphate, the spiritual authority of the Ottoman Empire, which was formally ended by Atatürk's secular Turkish government in 1924.

In fact, it is now generally thought that a large part of the Ottoman Empire's success was due to its relative tolerance towards Christians; indeed, it was its Christian subjects' preference for Ottoman rule that ensured the stability of the Empire. Orthodox and Protestant Christians, and also Jews, faced the prospect of forced conversion if they were 'liberated' by one of the many rivals of the Ottomans. The expression 'rather the Turkish turban than the Roman mitre' seems to have been common currency among the Empire's Christian subjects. The Ottoman rulers did not resort to forcible conversion because they were nicer than Christian rulers: non-Muslims could be charged an extra tax, so it made good economic sense to have a large pool of non-Muslim subjects. For the non-Muslim subjects, the tax was a burden which, however, brought stability and a fair degree of toleration.

The Islamist invocation of a restored Sunni 'Caliphate' has thus little to do with the original Ottoman Caliphate, and the best-known pan-Islamic group advocating restoration, Hizb ut-Tahrir, is banned in several Arab and western countries. The original Ottoman Empire, as the novelist Roderick Conway Morris has said, was 'from the outset a joint Muslim-Christian enterprise', with its founder Osman attracting as many (possibly more) Christians as Muslims in the late 13th century. The historian Caroline Finkel points out that 'coexistence and compromise. . . is one of the abiding themes of Ottoman history'. In today's world, however, 'coexistence and compromise' between Sunni fundamentalist rule on the one hand, and Muslim minorities and other faith groups (and secularists) on the other, is not very likely, and any such pan-Islamic regime would bear but scant resemblance to the Ottoman Caliphate.

There were two great slave trades in history

Slavery has been a part of human history since the earliest recorded times. In all known ancient civilizations, slaves were acquired by conquest and exploited as the owner saw fit.

What is now generally referred to as the 'Atlantic Slave Trade' began with Columbus when he exported Native American slaves to Europe (*see No one laughed at Christopher Columbus*). The transport soon began the other way, with European ships carrying African slaves to work and die in the Americas. The trade lasted from the 15th to the 19th centuries. For many people, the defining image of the Atlantic slave trade is still that shown in the TV series *Roots* (1977), with white raiders swooping on African villages. This is complete fiction. Providing slaves for the Atlantic trade was an African business: the white slavers could only ply their trade with the active cooperation of African slavers operating from coastal towns such as Badagry in Nigeria.

The Atlantic Slave Trade was enormous in scale: historian Hugh Thomas estimates that 13 million individuals were transported to the Americas across the Atlantic but millions died along the way. The Islamic slave trade in the Middle East is much less generally known, yet the numbers involved are equally vast. One estimate is that from the beginning of the Muslim era to the 20th century about 11.5 to 14 million Africans were sold into Islamic slavery in the Middle East (as with the Atlantic trade, many Africans died in the process of being gathered for sale as slaves). Saudi Arabia only abolished the slave trade in 1962.

Discussion of the two slave trades sometimes wanders into the frankly bizarre realm of debating the relative 'merits' of each trade. Thus it is said by some that black slaves in Islamic society have traditionally not been regarded in a racist manner (whatever comfort that might be for the slave), while others claim that slaves were preserved as valuable property in America (more cold comfort, no doubt). Though relatively seldom remarked upon, slavery still exists today, both in 'traditional' forms in some North African countries, and in the much more widespread form of bonded labour for loan 'repayment' (debts that can last for generations). See www.antislavery.org for some grim reading.

The Massacre of Glencoe was not that unusual (yet set a major legal precedent)

An inn in Glencoe had a sign saying that 'no Campbells or Hawkers' are to be served, something that causes most Scots more amusement than shame. The massacre (for massacre it undoubtedly was) took place on a cold February night in 1692, and was perpetrated by government troops billeted on the MacDonalds following their clan chief's late signing of an oath of allegiance to the new king, William of Orange. William himself signed the document calling for the MacDonalds of Glencoe to be 'extirpated'. Various unconvincing efforts have been made to exonerate William, who was in many respects a tolerant man, but the proclamation he signed was a death warrant.

The Civil War (*see Cromwell fought according to contemporary rules of war in Ireland*) had seen particularly fierce fighting in Scotland. Throughout the 1640s, bloody atrocities were inflicted on all sides, with the Campbells in the west suffering large-scale casualties among both combatants and non-combatants inflicted by Catholic Royalist forces, a hellish time the Campbells neither forgot nor forgave.

Also, following the Stuart Restoration in 1660, there was heavy persecution of Presbyterians in Scotland – the 'Killing Time', as the Covenanters dubbed the period. The accession of William in 1688 was seen by many Protestants not just as deliverance from persecution, but as a God-given chance to retaliate. The company sent to Glencoe will have included men whose family members had been butchered and raped by MacDonalds, and it was led by Robert Campbell, whose own land had been plundered by the Glencoe MacDonalds in 1689, while they were in retreat from the Battle of Dunkeld. These were still bloody times.

Campbell's orders read: 'You are hereby ordered to fall upon the rebels, MacDonalds of Glencoe, and put all to the sword under seventy. You are to have a special care that the old fox [the chief, MacIain] and his sons do upon no account escape your hands.' The butchery was soon over: 38 MacDonalds were killed, another 40 women and children fled and died in the hills. The killing would have been more comprehensive had other soldiers arrived in time: two of the approaching officers broke their swords rather than be party to the killing.

It is commonly said that the reason the massacre became so infamous so quickly was because it was a case of 'murder under trust', a breach of ancient Highland hospitality, but it is probable that the customs of Highland hospitality were not as rigorously observed in the real world as they were in the world of Walter Scott's novels. It was in truth the context of British politics that made the massacre widely known. What happened at Glencoe was far from being a unique event in Highland history. Several such horrific massacres, mini-genocides of minor clan branches, are known of, and lack of mercy to women and children was common practice.

The Glencoe Massacre was used as highly effective propaganda by Tory Jacobite sympathizers, and in 1695 the government set up an official Commission of Enquiry, which concluded that the Scottish Secretary, Sir John Dalrymple, was to blame. King William was of course found to be blameless, and there was a rapid adjustment of the historical record and reassignment of personnel: Campbell went off to war (and eventually died in poverty), others died in action, and Dalrymple was shunted out of the way for a bit (and eventually pardoned; he later far from contritely observed 'my only regret is that some of them escaped'). The king expressed his horror at the barbaric business, and thus Glencoe entered history and life moved on.

The Commission of Enquiry turned out to be of immense histori-cal importance, establishing in British law that 'no command against the laws of nature is binding; so that a soldier, retaining his commis-sion, ought to refuse to execute any barbarity', a judgment that set a vital precedent in world history.

Catherine the Great was not crushed to death by a horse

Catherine the Great was born a German princess in 1729; in 1745 she married the heir to the Russian throne and participated in a successful coup against her husband after he became Peter III. The unfortunate ex-tsar shortly thereafter died in an 'accident'; it seems one of Catherine's lovers, the splendidly named Count Orlov, stran-gled him.

As a woman ruler in an age when female rule was the exception, Catherine the Great came in for a great deal of public examination. She was quite certainly sexually active with many partners, if perhaps not as many as prurient speculation insisted upon. The long-held myth that she died with a horse on top of her is just nonsense, and is simply a crude reflection of male fear of a strong female leader. She died in 1796 of a stroke, in bed, aged 67.

The other great myth associated with her, that her minister Potem-kin built eponymous 'Potemkin villages', ie sham settlements filled with happy peasants for her to admire as she passed, only to be dis-mantled once she was out of sight, is almost certainly untrue, but the myth found an echo in the 20th century when tyrannies of both left and right constructed such settlements for the benefit of visitors.

Like her contemporary, Frederick the Great of Prussia, Catherine attracted intellectuals, and, also like Frederick, she was absurdly overpraised in particular by French writers, who loved the idea of malleable despots (malleable by intellectuals, and all for the com-mon good, of course). Diderot, Voltaire and Rousseau fluttered ex-citedly at her interest in their ideas, and she did in fact bring in some significant reforms in Russia. Her decision to be inoculated against smallpox not only worked its influence on Russian peasants, but on Europeans of all classes. Voltaire (whom she never met) called her the 'Star of the North'.

But enlightened or not, Catherine was an autocrat through and through. Her wars expanded Russian territory, her secret police were well nourished and people who threatened her reign were banished or killed. Like all autocrats, she was in truth a tyrant; she is a prophetic figure of the terrible monsters of modern times, monsters such as Stalin and Mao who could somehow charm thinkers with their self-proclaimed enlightened principles. This, and not the absurd sexual fantasies associated with her, is her main relevance today, as the first absolute ruler with professedly liberal support.

Casanova was a cross-dressing librarian

And his greatest love was a cross-dresser as well, though not a librarian. Casanova (1725-98) was many things before he ended up as a librarian in Count Waldstein's castle in Duchcov, but he was not, as some apologists have claimed, a modern sort of equal-opportunities lover. Indeed, his attitudes to women (he claimed 132 seductions) were not very modern at all. He was not in the least a proto-feminist and did not really care for independent women. He seems to have identified himself with Don Giovanni, seeing the Don's addiction to women as being the women's fault (Casanova knew Mozart and his librettist, Da Ponte, and may possibly have contributed to the opera's libretto). As well as being a lothario, he was a renowned author, a less renowned (obviously) spy, a banker, violinist, clergyman, physician and a soldier. He also invented the lottery. He had a reputation as a magician, was imprisoned in Venice for witchcraft (the Inquisition also pursued him) and seems to have known everybody of consequence in the latter part of the 18th century.

In July 1749 he met his great love, a somewhat mysterious French-woman called Henriette. Their affair lasted until February 1750 when she returned to her family. Casanova was depressed by the end of the affair, the saddest moment of his life according to his autobiography, and took refuge in freemasonry. Henriette – who may well have been, like Casanova, some kind of spy – liked to pass herself off as a castrato, and frequently dressed as a man. Casanova himself liked to dress as a woman later in life, which is what seems to have led some scholars to the conclusion that he identified with women, but it is a tenuous inference. A psychological distinction has often been drawn between 'Don Juans', who simply add conquests, and 'Casanovas', who just like women a lot, but Casanova was in these terms very much a 'Don Juan' (Henriette perhaps excepted).

Casanova wrote 12 volumes of memoirs and it is fair to say that his descriptions of his amours – in the original or in translation – are pretty feeble by the standards of other 18th-century writers such as John Cleland. Cleland's *Fanny Hill* (1749) is of course fiction, and the memoirs are (purportedly) fact, but Cleland does usually at least give the impression of two people being present during coition. Casanova witters on in schoolboy fashion about 'ebony fleeces' and the like, whereas Cleland gets, as it were, to the point.

General Napier did not wire 'peccavi' home to England

General Sir Charles Napier became commander-in-chief of the British forces in India in 1842 and led an army against the rebellious province of Sindh (now the southernmost part of Pakistan), which he captured in 1843. A popular myth has it that Napier then sent back to England the one word 'peccavi', Latin for 'I have sinned', therefore 'I have Sindh'.

It is a lovely story but completely untrue. For a start, the telegraph was quite new in those days and there was no telegraphic connection between India and England. And Napier didn't think of it: it was in fact a 17-year-old girl in England who came up with it. She told her father, who wrote to *Punch* magazine on 18 March 1844, who gleefully publicized the jest (not as a cartoon, as is often said). The girl in question is reputed by some to have been Catherine Winkworth (1827-78), who subsequently became a noted translator of Lutheran hymns.

Napier was a complex man with a sharp wit. He had earlier written in his private journal for 1838: 'We have no right to seize Sindh yet we shall do so, and a very advantageous, useful, humane piece of rascality it will be.' A delegation of Hindu officials once approached him after he banned 'suttee', the practice of burning widows on their husband's funeral pyres. The officials explained that this was their custom, and Napier explained that it was his country's custom to

> ## Not in so many words
>
> "Money is the root of all evil." The actual words in the King James Bible (1 Timothy 6.10) are "For the love of money is the root of all evil".

hang men who burned women alive – an early example of the limits of multiculturalism.

There are a few apocryphal tales similar to the 'peccavi' story. One is that when Lord Dalhousie annexed Oudh in 1856, he said 'vovi' (I have vowed). Another famous pun is attributed to Sir Walter Raleigh, who is supposed to have said of the routed Spanish Armada in 1588, 'cantharides' (Spanish fly). Sadly, neither of these fables is true.

There was nothing Thatcherite about Maggie's 'Victorian values' – Flashman is nearer the mark

In January 1983 the prime minister Margaret Thatcher began talking admiringly about 'Victorian Values', which she claimed were true British values. Though never concisely defined by Mrs Thatcher, they were clearly a mixture of economic, moral and ethical principles: hard work was fundamental and self-help was also basic (though Samuel Smiles may not have liked the Thatcher version of this concept), as were stable (usually patriarchal) family life, respect for authority and for established religion and a reverence for things as they are. Maggie's reverence for 'Victorian Values' also extended to the arts. In her autobiography, perhaps with Lytton Strachey's *Eminent Victorians* (1918) in mind, she is quite sniffy about what she sees as 'Bloomsbury' values, a tendency as she saw it to sneer at 'real' (ie wealth-creating) people and politics.

Thatcher's expression was very quickly and gleefully adopted throughout the English-speaking world, especially in Reagan's America, but dissent from the view that Victorian principles lay behind 'Thatcherism' and free-market monetarism was also forthcoming. As many commentators have pointed out, the Victorians were actually keen on large-scale publicly funded works with communal ends in view, works which were meant to last. We still depend on

145

Victorian reservoirs and sewers, fine practical examples of what the historian David Marquand calls the 'distinct, self-conscious and vigorous public domain', in *Decline of the Public* (2004).

The phrase 'Victorian Values' had actually been used six months prior to Thatcher's speech, in a review by historian David Cannadine's of *Flashman and the Redskins* (1982), the latest instalment of George MacDonald Fraser's marvellous series of novels about the archetypal British bounder Sir Harry Flashman (1822-1915). Cannadine, however, was pointing out that the Flashman saga 'took the lid off Victorian values'. Flashman's life is 'lived wholly at variance with its carapace of virtuous achievement and public recognition' – his cynical view of the imperial enterprise, it should be noted, is not so different from that of genuine heroes (*see* **General Napier did not wire 'peccavi' home to England**). The final twist is that the monstrously self-seeking Flashman would have been quite at home with Thatcherite values. In the sharpest of 1980s clothes and toting the latest brick-sized mobile phone, Sir Harry would be a fitting companion for Harry Enfield's 'Loadsamoney'.

Oral history can be bunk

The skeleton of 'Kennewick Man' was discovered in 1996 in Kennewick, Washington. According to an Act passed by Congress in 1990, Native American groups can claim ownership of human remains if they can prove a link with the remains, and this proof can include 'oral traditions'. The Act has been vigorously disputed by museums who say they must be allowed to examine historically important human remains, and equally vigorously defended by Native Americans, who say it is a vital part of their religious practice to honour the bones of their dead ancestors by reinterring them with appropriate ceremony. Kennewick Man is especially interesting because he is virtually complete and is very old (around 8,400 years old in fact), and his relation to any modern tribal grouping is debatable.

Also debatable is the weight of oral tradition here. 'Kennewick Man' has been dubbed the 'Ancient One' by some Native American activists ('someone that we cherish as one of our own') and it is claimed by some that reliable oral traditions go back to his time. How reliable can such traditions be? Historian A J P Taylor once notoriously dismissed oral history as 'old men drooling about their youth'. For those who sympathize with the modern plight of many Native American tribes (though some are doing very well), the temptation to side against Taylor and take even the furthest-stretching claims for oral history seriously is strong, but...

Many if not most Native American memories of what happened at the Battle of the Little Big Horn in 1876 were collected soon after the battle, and if oral history is reliable then these accounts should surely cohere. The US authorities had a strong interest in finding out what happened, as of course did the victors. The Lakota (and Cheyenne) testimonies are in fact all over the place, which is authentic enough (that is what battle memories are like – on one part of the field a group can be sharing a pot of tea, while 500 yards away men are disembowelling each other). The Lakota called this particular battle the 'Greasy Grass Fight'. It lasted something between 20 and 30 minutes. In most versions the troopers fought well, but in others they were cowards, and so forth. The accounts vary widely and show little agreement on what happened (except about who won).

The western discipline of archaeology is gradually giving up the secrets of Greasy Grass. We know where the final fighting took place; we know, too, that the troopers were in awful physical condition. They must have looked pretty rough, though no Lakota testimony tells us this. Archaeology verifies some Lakota accounts and refutes others, and this is as it should be. Memory studies are fascinating: at any given point, perhaps 5% of our memories have been invented by our own busy little brain. People clearly remember things that cannot possibly have happened (in one famous case, subjects confidently remembered implanted memories of seeing Bugs Bunny – a Warner Bros character – at Disneyland) and stress will encourage the memory to make one's own role in actual events more impressive, whether in a playground scuffle or before the walls of Troy. Add generational boasting to this process and it's a wonder anything true survives. Western historians in general, however, no longer despise oral history, and usually see it as a useful adjunct to the written and archaeological records. The archaeologists can tell us which body was Sergeant Butler's, but the Lakota witnesses agree about his bravery, and no archaeologist can tell us that.

The past is an imaginary country

As L P Hartley said, they do things differently in the past, perhaps nowhere more differently than in themed historical attractions, where actors dress up in costumes and act as the originals are supposed to have acted – at least in the historically approved view. One of the most surreal of such attractions is the recreation of 18th-century colonial Williamsburg, in Virginia. It consists of a 301-acre 'Historical Area' in which the visitor can view reconstructed buildings such as the Capitol and the House of Burgesses, quaff ale from tankards in warm taverns, converse with white actors with 'Ole Virginny' accents and, of course, spend money in the 'fine and varied' shops.

The most startling thing about the Williamsburg attraction is the absence of black faces. The real colonial Williamsburg would have had black people everywhere, mainly doing menial tasks. Such historical accuracy would be unpalatable in modern America, so the past is rewritten. While quite understandable, this is bonkers as a reconstruction of old Virginia. Reconstructions of slave life in the US are also very difficult. As historian David Lowenthal has pointed out, watermelons were commonly consumed in the past by slaves, but are not eaten in the reinvented past as they appear to truckle to a notorious stereotype.

Much is made of the revolutionary Patrick Henry at Williamsburg. Visitors are invited to sit on the straight-backed benches at the reconstructed Capitol and imagine the ringing speeches of Patrick Henry and 'the courageous Virginia planters and tradesmen who risked all for principle'. They didn't of course risk 'all'. No one believed for a moment the British would or could execute all who opposed them, and in any case by no means all of those heroic slaveholders sitting on the 'straight-backed benches' were for revolution. As for Patrick Henry, the only speech any of his contemporaries thought worth recording (in 1765) did have a good slap at George III, but the effect was spoiled by a fast apology. The only evidence for his famous 'Give me liberty or give me death' speech is from an 1817 biography of dubious authority.

Williamsburg represents an imaginary past, but it's not just pasts that can be invented. 20th-century communist regimes delighted in creating imaginary presents for foreign visitors to see, industrious and happy little communities that were shut down as soon as the gullible westerners passed by. Religious groups have always created imaginary futures for martyrs to look forward to when they die: Iranian Shia boy soldiers marched over minefields during the Iran-Iraq war with little gold-coloured plastic keys that would let them into Paradise pinned to their jackets, and Sunni suicide bombers attacking Shia mosques in Pakistan and Iraq are also no doubt told their actions lead straight to Paradise. An imaginary future need not be for oneself, and can be wholly secular: many thousands of communist troops, for example, have died confident of oblivion for themselves and a better future for their people.

History – 20th Century

Stalin stayed in a doss house in London's East End (but Lenin and Trotsky did not)

Throughout the 1990s, foreign governments accused the British government of sheltering Islamic extremists in 'Londonistan'. The suggestion was made, indeed, that some kind of dark deal had been done between the extremists and the British government that they could live here provided they didn't engage in terrorist acts. The idea that Islamic extremists have some sort of negotiating body to speak on their behalf is a concept that would appeal to cartoonists and to the CIA, but the 'extremists' are often comic-opera figures. The trick is to identify the genuinely scary individuals among those who circle around such figures.

We have been here before. Joseph Conrad's novel, *The Secret Agent* (1907), brings to life a world of exiles and extremists that reads uncannily like our own world. London in the late Victorian and Edwardian periods was full of exiled liberals, socialists, communists, anarchists, spies and murderers. The East End of London had a large Jewish community, which itself hosted many revolutionaries. The Siege of Sidney Street in 1911, during which a gang of anarchists-cum-robbers led by 'Peter the Painter' (Peter Piatkov) killed three policemen, can be seen as a dramatic end to that period. Three years later, the world changed dramatically. Despite a foul statement by General Kitchener – as Margot Asquith said, not a great man, but a great poster – that he did not want Jews in the army, the Jews of the East End signed up in their thousands.

Lenin and Trotsky first met in London in 1902. In 1907, Stalin made a trip to London to attend the 5th Congress of the Russian Social Democratic Party in Whitechapel Road, with Lenin and Trotsky also in attendance. Stalin lodged (for 6d a night) at Tower House in Fieldgate St, an oddly oppressive building that still stands, and was described by the novelist Jack London (who had some experience in these matters) as a 'Monster Doss House'. It is often claimed that Trotsky and Lenin stayed in the doss house also, to display solidarity with the workers, but it seems unlikely that either of them would have been able or willing to waste much time on such gesture politics. Trotsky had plenty of people to stay with, and Lenin liked to be in Bloomsbury, near the British Library, so the idea of the three of them cosily dossing down together among the fleas is almost certainly just a socialist urban myth.

There were no Angels of Mons

The so-called 'Angels of Mons' story (often a singular angel) was very quickly demonstrated to be bogus, but remains terribly tenacious and is one of the best-documented examples of a myth quickly taking hold. In September 1914 the *London Evening News* published a story by Arthur Machen called 'The Bowmen', in which, during the Battle of Mons on 23 August, the ghosts of dead English archers (killed at the Battle of Agincourt in 1415) come to the rescue of the British Expeditionary Force and kill enough of the Germans to allow the British to retreat safely (why they didn't kill enough of the Germans to let the British win is unexplained).

Within weeks of the story being published it had been accepted as fact by large numbers of people (including, it seems, soldiers who had been in the fighting), despite Machen's increasingly desperate assertions that he made the whole thing up. Later, there was even a popular 'Angel of Mons' waltz. Machen had described the bowmen as 'shining', and clergymen began calling the bowmen angels in their sermons. Machen said: 'in the popular view shining and benevolent supernatural beings are angels and nothing else… and so, I believe, the Bowmen of my story have become the Angels of Mons.' Machen also correctly identified the process by which such stories are passed on as fact: 'someone (unknown) has met a nurse (unnamed) who has talked to a soldier (anonymous) who has seen angels. But THAT is not evidence'.

To Machen's fury, people began claiming that he had taken a true first-hand account from a witness and had turned it into fiction. Harold Begbie's *On the Side of the Angels* (1915), which went through at least four printings, provided what it claimed were 'eyewitness' accounts (one of which at least was a blatant hoax), adding, as a killer argument, that Machen may well have received 'telepathic' messages from soldiers at the front.

'The Bowmen' is not actually a terribly good story and rates pretty low in Machen's occult fiction, which includes that disturbing masterpiece *The Three Impostors* (1895). Machen's introduction to the 1923 edition of this book describes how a clergyman suggested to him that the very improbable events in the book were true, and this prompted him to think that his imaginings 'may suggest the probable existence of a world very far and remote from the world of common experience. It may turn out after all that the weavers of fantasy are the veritable realists'. Or, of course, he could just have got fed up of pointing out he was a fiction writer.

British WWI generals were neither fools nor sadists

Thanks to television, cinema and popular history, the one secure lesson the British learn from history is that the British forces in WWI were led by men who were fools at best and criminal sadists at worst. Stephen Fry's portrait of a British general in *Blackadder* – arrogant, cowardly, safely living in luxury behind the lines while the men in the trenches die in squalor – is a typical example. The process of questioning the motives and talents of the European leaders began quickly after the war, and the late 20s saw the publication of memoirs such as Robert Graves's *Goodbye to All That* and novels such as Erich Maria Remarque's *All Quiet on the Western Front*; but though the disillusion was Europe-wide, it seems to be the British who have mainly bought into the myth (as for the Americans, General Pershing has never been anything but a hero).

By 1929, the year of Graves's and Remarque's books, communists, fascists and liberals had all agreed the war had been a 'Bad Thing': for communists it showed the workers could be deluded into fighting each other; for German fascists it showed the enemy was within stabbing the nation in the back; for British liberals it was all a huge waste of humanity – we had all stumbled into war and fought it badly. Wilfred Owen's poem 'Futility' expresses the sense of waste perfectly: 'Was it for this the clay grew tall?'

Yet it was a war fought for clearly defined aims by each protagonist, and the facts do not bear out the popular notion of a leadership of bumbling cowards. At least 58 British generals were killed in action, and many more were wounded. As for incompetence, during the so-called 'Hundred Days' in 1918 the British won a long succession of victories that led to the end of the war. The war was attritional and horrendous in terms of loss of human life, but it is arguable that it was fought with more restraint (and proportionally fewer casualties if civilian deaths are included) than an earlier war which was also fought with barbed wire and machine guns, the American Civil War. Probably no British general, for example, would have led a campaign such as Sherman's scorched-earth 'March to the Sea' in Georgia; proof also perhaps of the old perception that wars within nations are fiercer than wars between nations.

➣ *See also **The British did not betray the Anzacs at Gallipoli**.*

The British did not betray the Anzacs at Gallipoli

The belief that the Anzacs (Australian and New Zealand WWI forces) were betrayed at Gallipoli by an incompetent British officer class (*see also **British WWI generals were neither fools nor sadists***) is still a popular orthodoxy but is not regarded as true by serious historians. There are actually two enduring myths about Gallipoli. The first is that the assault force on the Turkish peninsula of Gallipoli in 1915 (its aim being to capture Constantinople and open the Dardanelles to Allied shipping) was composed largely of antipodean troops.

The British were in fact the largest contingent and the British troops suffered the heaviest casualties: the death toll was 21,255 British, 9,798 French, 8,709 Australians, 2,701 New Zealanders, 1,358 Indian soldiers (Sikhs and Gurkhas) and 49 Newfoundlanders. Turkish casualties were enormous, about 300,000, of whom around 90,000 were killed. A large proportion of the Anzacs were in fact recent immigrants, who regarded themselves very much as British. Indeed, many Anzac troops actually landed wearing British-style headgear, but the official Australian painter of the battle, George Lambert, was ordered to paint them for posterity with slouch hats on.

The second myth, that the British took a back seat during the fighting, which maintains its sticking power in modern times thanks largely to Peter Weir's film *Gallipoli* (1981), is altogether more insidious, and forms the basis of much current popular opinion of the campaign. It didn't help that British historians drew attention to every flaw in the campaign, and that even the official British war historian deliberately played down the British role and was reluctant to even *imply* any criticism of the Anzac forces. This doubtless prepared the ground for Weir's film, which shows British troops in a very unflattering light compared to the heroic Anzac forces.

Gallipoli was partly sponsored by Rupert Murdoch. Murdoch's father, Keith Murdoch, had played a key part in creating the picture of helpless Anzacs at the mercy of inept British senior officers. As the journalist Les Carlyon has shown, Murdoch senior's uncensored and damning report on the campaign, which was circulated in influential quarters in London, actually had true things to say; but the truth was muddled up with falsity and a somewhat camp contrast between the manly Australian soldiers 'swinging their fine limbs' and the British 'toy soldiers'.

Peter Weir's film was one of the first major films for Mel Gibson, who has made a career of (to adapt Noel Coward) 'being beastly to the English'. The myth of the cowardly English at Gallipoli prevails alas, and is a dreadful insult to the memory of brave men.

Not in so many words

"Pride goes before a fall." The correct wording from the King James Bible (Proverbs 16.18) is "Pride goeth before destruction, and an haughty spirit before a fall".

Japan treated prisoners of war very well (in WWI)

Soon after WWII ended, Japan came to be seen by western governments as an ally against communism and there emerged a strong desire, particularly on the part of the USA, to bury memories of the bitter war between Japan and the Allies. Much of liberal opinion in the west was perhaps less interested in the political alliance against the communist world, and was more concerned with projecting Japan as a society much like ours and not an alien culture. In that sense, both liberals and anti-communists had the same agenda. Japan's place in the modern world essentially mirrored that of Lt Sulu in *Star Trek*, happily mixing with other races under American hegemony; liberals could see a multiracial future, imperialists could see unlimited expansion.

The Japanese treatment of Allied prisoners during WWII was a problem for this unlikely consensus, with very few former prisoners of the Japanese being willing to either forgive or forget their horrendous treatment. The common apology for the brutal treatment of prisoners was that the Japanese fighting code did not allow for prisoners. The very concept was alien, samurai warriors would choose 'death before dishonour', it was a clash of cultures and so forth. It was all very unfortunate, agreed all sides, but perhaps inevitable given such different cultural views.

The problem with this explanation-cum-rehabilitation is that it isn't true in any respect. There was no part of any so-called 'samurai code' that forbade surrender. Samurai regularly surrendered, ceasefires were often negotiated and safe passage was given, and samurai prisoners of war were treated no better and no worse than in western societies. And the treatment given to German prisoners during WWI and to Russians during the 1905 Russo-Japanese war was quite splendid; indeed, Japan had a reputation for how well it treated enemy prisoners before its entry into WWII. Enlisted men were treated practically as guests, officers could even be sent to a Buddhist retreat for relaxation and recuperation.

Why did the dramatic change occur in WWII? There are lots of arguments, but the likeliest is simply that the Japanese leaders believed they were certain to win and could do what they liked. The treatment of non-Westerners was much, much worse. The 1937-8 Rape of Nanking (still not really accepted as historical fact in Japan) by Japanese soldiers was one of the most terrible war crimes in history, yet Japan suffered no serious political consequences at the time. The point was evidently taken by Japanese leaders. (Ironically, one of the westerners who did most to try to protect Chinese civilians was a Nazi official, John Rabe).

Not all swastikas are bad

Since the Nazis adopted the swastika in 1920, it has been seen as an unequivocal signifier of evil. The form of the Nazi swastika was laid down by Hitler in *Mein Kampf* and was proclaimed by the Nazis to be an ancient symbol of 'Aryan' culture (it was already in use by German rightists before Hitler). The swastika is defined by Chambers as 'a Greek cross with arms bent at a right angle, esp. clockwise'. The 'fylfot' version of the swastika has truncated arms and is often turned anti-clockwise. There are in fact many variants of the swastika form and 'fylfot' is now commonly used as a non-contentious synonym, especially when describing its use in design and heraldry.

The swastika is a very ancient and almost commonplace sign in many cultures, and versions of it similar to the modern one go back to at least 2000 BC. It has long been used as a good and beneficent symbol in many religions (Rudyard Kipling had the swastika as an essential part of the design on his works). It appears frequently in Hindu ritual (especially during lamplighting in Diwali) and also has a long history in Buddhism, but is most identified with Jainism. Jain temples must have swastikas, which means that attempts to ban the swastika in Europe, as has been proposed by some politicians, is a non-starter (the Falun Gong also use it).

For many years in the 20th century there was a Swastika Laundry in Dublin, which had an enormous swastika on its building and on its vans. The German writer Heinrich Böll, visiting Dublin in 1955, was apparently so shocked by the sight of a Swastika Laundry van he was almost run over by one while staring at it.

The swastika can give offence in unexpected ways. A noted example was Prince Harry's wearing of a swastika armband on an Afrika Korps uniform at a fancy dress party, which offended for all the usual reasons. However, it was also claimed to be offensive to at least some Afrika Korps veterans, as it was a symbol some units did not choose to emphasize. On the other hand, there were many Afrika Korps units which happily used the symbol (the British desire to see the Afrika Korps as 'gallant' non-Nazis was largely self-deluding, and harks back to earlier desert myths of supposed chivalric conflict between Crusaders and Saracens).

Mussolini did not make the trains run on time

The claim that Italian dictator Benito Mussolini 'made the trains run on time' has become an almost proverbial phrase acknowledging that good can come out of bad: the flood destroyed your crop, but replenished the aquifer; you caught an infection but it has given you resistance, and so on.

It seems plausible enough at first. After Mussolini became prime minister in 1922 (assuming full dictatorial powers in 1925) he took personal control of much of Italian public life. Trains were highly symbolic beasts in the 1920s for both communists and fascists; they connected the country, increased control of remote areas and looked fabulous on the great propaganda posters of the 1920s. Being seen to make the trains run on time was a given of authoritarian rule, a rule enforced by a new breed of official. Hemingway and other contemporary observers wrote, usually admiringly, of the 'New Man' being created by Mussolini's Italian fascism: efficient, incorruptible and not to be messed with. The same 'New Man' was also of course being identified by visitors to the Soviet Union (the expression was to resurface in the 1980s as a marketing term for supposedly non-sexist men).

It is perhaps possible to overstate the case that Mussolini deserves no credit for making Italy's trains run on time, if only for the satisfaction of puncturing a myth, but the truth is that much of Europe's railway system was in difficulty after WWI ended, and Italy's railway system in particular could only improve, and needed to improve quickly. The trains got better, but they were getting better everywhere, and in Italy's case the reconstruction work began before Mussolini's accession to power.

Rail users everywhere are a notoriously querulous bunch, but there is plenty of contemporary evidence to suggest that Italian commuters were generally not happy with the supposedly wondrous new fascist system.

Hitler did not snub Jesse Owens at the 1936 Berlin Olympics

The story that Hitler snubbed Jesse Owens varies a bit, but occurs mostly in this form: at the 1936 Berlin Olympics, the American black athlete Jesse Owens won four gold medals, and Hitler was so outraged at a black man winning races ahead of white Aryan athletes that he stormed out of the stadium. Owens indeed beat white athletes and won an unprecedented four golds – a feat not matched by a black athlete until Carl Lewis in 1984 – but the other elements of the story are just hooey.

In fact, as Owens stated in his autobiography *The Jesse Owens Story* (1970), Hitler did not storm out of the stadium at the end of any of Owens's victories. Instead, Hitler gave Owens what seems suspiciously like a cheery wave: 'When I passed the Chancellor he arose, waved his hand at me, and I waved back at him. I think the writers showed bad taste in criticizing the man of the hour in Germany.' Not only that, the Berlin crowd gave Owens huge ovations every time he won, and Leni Riefenstahl (Hitler's favourite director) gave Owens equal status with white athletes in her film of the Olympics. Hitler did indeed snub a black American athlete: Cornelius Johnson won a medal on the first day, and Hitler left the stadium just before the award; his underlings insisted a prior arrangement was in place, but no one believed this then or now. Just why he should snub Johnson and not Owens is not known; pontificators on Hitler sometimes forget he was not an entirely rational person.

Over the years Owens simply gave up trying to put the story right; the myth has been just too strong, and survives in reference books into the 21st century. The older Owens grew, the more tenacious became the myth, perhaps because the myth hides a much more sinister truth, an unpleasant truth about America itself. When Owens returned to America, President Roosevelt refused to meet him, as the honouring of a black man in mid-30s America would be unpalatable to the public, especially in the South. As Owens later observed, it was Roosevelt, not Hitler, who snubbed him; and never again, as a competitor, did Owens receive the public acclaim from an audience comparable to that Berlin gave him in 1936; he was reduced to being a freak show, racing against horses, and ended up a jazz DJ.

➤ *See also* **Hitler was not a vegetarian.**

Fascist Spain protected Jews during WWII

The Spanish dictator General Franco has had a bad press, even by fascist dictator standards. In the 1930s he won a cruelly fought civil war against the Spanish government (with help from Hitler, whose pilots learned how to bomb and strafe civilians in Spain) and established a viciously repressive regime that lasted until 1975.

Yet, odd as it seems, Franco's Spain was a refuge for many European Jews. Franco did protect Sephardic Jews (ie Iberian or North African Jews) throughout Nazi-occupied Europe. A 1924 Spanish law gave any European Jew who could prove Sephardic ancestry the right to apply for a Spanish passport.

A study by Chaim Lipschitz, *Franco, Spain, The Jews and the Holocaust* (1984) claims that as many as 45,000 Jews were saved by Spain from Nazi-occupied Europe, and it has also been claimed that Franco refused to send back German Jewish refugees, on the legalistic ground that as the Nazis did not recognize them as citizens, they had no right to have them back. Lipschitz's claim that Franco should be seen as a 'protector' has not surprisingly been challenged: there is evidence that Franco was disparaging towards Jews. Yet even those who challenge Lipschitz accept that Franco's regime gave refuge to thousands of Jews, and protected thousands of others, notably in Hungary, where Spanish papers were much sought after.

The significant comparison is of course with the attitude of the European democracies towards Jewish refugees. Ireland, for example, placed many barriers to entry; it was indicated that applicants should be Catholic converts, and also wealthy. In the end, Ireland took in perhaps as few as 30-70 Jewish refugees, most certainly an appallingly low number. Irish politicians, the Irish media and Church figures were openly anti-semitic, often venomously so. In 1945 the Irish President, Eamon de Valera, passed the condolences of the Irish people to the German ambassador when he heard of Hitler's death. This has been dismissed by some as merely an officious demonstration of Irish neutrality, but it looks somewhat darker in the context of Ireland's refusal to take refugees from Hitler (George Bernard Shaw's description of de Valera's action as an act of 'Christian chivalry' has sometimes been taken seriously, but must surely be a macabre joke).

Franco is of course a safe target, in the sense that he could certainly have done more and is no longer a live issue. But the history of the democracies in relation to the Holocaust, perhaps particularly that of Ireland, is still a live issue, and an altogether pricklier one.

The real Charlotte Grays are far more interesting than the fictional version

Sebastian Faulks' novel *Charlotte Gray* (1999) was generally well reviewed, though the film version (2001) was not much liked. The film was criticized for its supposed overly heroic, indeed melodramatic, mood and plot, but this latter aspect was realistic enough – the true stories of the female agents sent into Nazi-occupied France were often melodramatic in nature, but also truly heroic, with many of the stories, inevitably, having tragic endings.

The Special Operations Executive was set up by the British government to work with local Resistance movements and 'to set Europe ablaze'. SOE sent 470 agents into Europe, 39 of whom were women, and over 200 of these agents were killed. The female agents included Violette Szabo, Odette and Princess Noor Khan.

Violette Szabo is perhaps the best-known of all SOE agents, following her portrayal by Virginia McKenna in the movie *Carve Her Name with Pride* (1958). Szabo's French husband was killed at El Alamein in 1942 (their daughter was born that year); she was sent into France in 1944. The radio cipher given to her by cryptographer Leo Marks is a now much-anthologized poem which begins:

The life that I have
Is all that I have
And the life that I have is yours

She was finally captured after a fierce gun battle (she had been captured and escaped before – twice), then severely tortured and murdered by the Gestapo in Ravensbrück in 1945, aged 23.

Odette Sansom also had a film made of her exploits: *Odette* (1950), starring Anna Neagle. She was betrayed and arrested in 1943; like Violette and virtually all other captured agents, she was mercilessly tortured (her toenails were pulled out) and sent to Ravensbrück; she survived the war, dying in 1992 at the age of 82. She gave her occupation in *Who's Who* as 'housewife'.

The most unusual SOE agent, and surely one of the most unorthodox spies of all time, was Princess Noor Khan, a descendant of Tipu Sultan, the 'Tiger of Mysore' (South India's last Muslim ruler, who died fighting the Duke of Wellington). Noor Khan was born in the Kremlin and brought up in England and France. She was a devout Sufi, and was related through her mother to Mary Baker Eddy, the founder of Christian Science. Her big drawback as a spy was that she could not tell a lie; once, during training, while carrying a radio on her bike, she was stopped by a policeman and calmly informed him she was training to be a spy. She actually lasted longer in the field than most other agents and was apparently finally betrayed to the Gestapo by a woman jealous of her beauty. After suffering much brutality for a year (she refused to give information), she was murdered with three other SOE agents in Dachau in 1944; she was 30, and her last words were 'Vive la liberté'.

The Times crossword did not give D-day codewords as solutions

This remarkable coincidence is sometimes associated with *The Times* in popular culture, perhaps because it was seen as the paper of the Establishment, but the crosswords in question actually appeared in *The Daily Telegraph*. It is a very odd story, but the fact that many codewords did appear as *Telegraph* crossword answers in the build-up to D-day has never been in dispute.

Churchill and Roosevelt agreed in January 1943 that the long called-for 'Second Front' against the Nazis (to support the first being held by the USSR) should happen and preparations for a landing in northern France began soon after. The planning was of course top secret, and officials who let the slightest operational hints fall were demoted or discharged. In May 1944, just a month before the D-day landings were scheduled to take place, Britain's Intelligence Service noticed that operational codewords for the landing were appearing in the very popular *Daily Telegraph* crossword. The answer to one clue was 'Utah', and another answer was 'Omaha'. These were the names given to the beaches in Normandy where the American Forces were to land on D-day. Other answers included: 'Mulberry', the ultra-secret British floating harbours that were to be set up for landing supplies after the invasion; 'Neptune', code for Royal Navy support; and perhaps the most dramatic answer of all, 'Overlord', the name for the entire invasion operation itself. The codenames for the British and Canadian beaches, 'Gold', 'Sword' and 'Juno', had appeared in previous months.

The obvious fear was that someone had been passing codenames to the compiler, and the compiler was using the *Telegraph* crossword to pass on information to the Nazis. Two British agents descended upon the man responsible for the crosswords, a teacher called Leonard Dawe, who lived in Leatherhead, Surrey. Dawe insisted the clues and answers had no hidden meaning.

The affair is generally cited as an example of how something seemingly meaningful can occur wholly randomly, but the answers may perhaps not have been quite so coincidental. It has been occasionally claimed that Dawe invited schoolboys into his study and encouraged them to find interesting words for him, and that one of the boys got the words from hanging around local army bases. Perhaps a definitive account will emerge one day.

> **❝**
> ### Not in so many words
> "Religion is the opium of the people." What Marx actually wrote was "Religion is the sigh of the oppressed creature, the heart of a heartless world and the soul of soulless conditions. It is the opium of the people." In context it is clear that Marx was not saying that religion is a tool for drugging the masses, as is often assumed, but rather that it makes appalling conditions bearable.
> **❞**

D-day was a hard fight for all the Allies

It's very unfortunate, of course, but the British and the French agree on one thing, that the American Army had it easy during WWII. Why this should be so may be down to jealousy of how well-supplied the Americans were, what snazzy uniforms they wore, or their unlimited supply of cigarettes and stockings; it certainly owes nothing to the facts (the Canadians had all those plus points too, but were never despised). The Americans fought hard and well from 1944 onwards. and in some of the most brutal of the Western campaigns. Spielberg's *Saving Private Ryan* (1998) is a quite accurate picture of the reception the Americans got on Omaha Beach on 6 June 1944. Operation Overlord was massive: over 5,000 ships (backed up by 11,500 planes) to get more than 150,000 men up 20 yards of beach.

As if to make up for the disdain of the Allies, many American accounts practically write everyone else out of the script (except for the Germans of course, and only because an enemy is needed, one assumes). There is one snide reference to General Montgomery in *Saving Private Ryan*, which is fairly representative of how many Americans see the British on D-day. On the real D-day, the Americans landed 73,000 men, the British 62,000 and the Canadians 22,000. Perhaps surprisingly, there is no official casualty rate for D-day and all figures are estimates.

The US casualties totalled around 6,600, over a third of whom were from their airborne forces, and around 2,000 on Omaha beach. The American share of the casualties for D-day is more than high enough to put European contempt to shame, but the manufacturers of American popular culture such as Spielberg should also be ashamed: the Americans did not die alone that day. The British took 2,000 casualties on Gold and Sword beaches (the same as the US at Omaha), and British airborne troops were heavily hit: around 600 killed or wounded, 600 more missing (the 'missing' here usually means dead). The Canadians at Juno Beach suffered around 1,000 casualties. With all these figures, approximately a quarter to one third will be actual deaths, the remainder including wounded, missing or captured.

The feeling that the Americans were not overstrained during WWII is possibly down to a sense that the USA had not suffered like the other Allies. In that great and still controversial movie *The Victors* (1963), an American detachment prepares to accept the surrender of a small German force. A French outfit approaches and fires on the Germans, so they will continue to fight and therefore be killed. The smiling French officer explains to the Americans that of course they were never occupied. This contrast between American innocence and European experience is of course an old theme of American fiction.

Lady Astor did not call the British troops in Italy 'D-day Dodgers'

Not long after D-day, 6 June 1944, a rumour emerged among the British forces fighting in Italy that the MP, Lady Astor, had called them 'D-day Dodgers', implying that they were men who were shirking from the real action in northern France. Lady Astor was a Tory, an American, a famous teetotaller and of course a woman, so the British troops were quite prepared to believe the worst. The British forces in Italy, particularly the 8th Army, had being having a tough time of it (the present author's father, who was wounded in North Africa, was one of them; he hated Lady Astor for the rest of his life). The North African and Italian campaigns were hard fought: by the time the rumour appeared, the British had fought their way from El Alamein, through Sicily, Salerno and Anzio and up the spine of Italy.

Shortly after the rumour had become established as fact in the minds of the soldiers, a song appeared and also spread quickly. The title was the 'D-day Dodgers', to the tune of 'Lili Marlene', and the song was one of the best of WWII, indeed of any war. The final stanza – there are small variants – confirms that it was written by a genius:

> Look around the mountains
> In the mud and rain,
> You'll find the scattered crosses,
> Some which bear no name.
> Heartbreak and toil and suffering gone
> The lads beneath, they slumber on,
> They are the D-day Dodgers,
> Who stayed in Italy.

This genius was quite possibly the British intelligence officer Hamish Henderson, poet, singer and communist, whose best-known work is *Elegies for the Dead in Cyrenaica* (1948). Henderson certainly 'collected' a version, but as with Sir Walter Scott and the ballads, how much is original and how much 'shaped' may never be known. It was certainly very personal to him – according to Henderson's *Guardian* obituary in 2002, he cried when former Labour Minister Denis Healey (who had been a beachmaster on D-day) sang it on television.

But great though the song is, it is in fact a slander against a fine woman. Lady Astor never said any such thing. It would contradict all that we know of her, and no one has ever come up with the slightest evidence that she ever said anything at all derogatory about any British soldiers. So how did the rumour start? It may have just grown from an idle comment, but it is possible that there is a darker source, and that the rumour may have been started by Italian or German Intelligence, and is thus a masterstroke of black propaganda. If true, this would unfortunately mean that in singing the song and asserting the Astor story as fact, socialist folk singers have been peddling fascist propaganda since the 1940s.

Tokyo Rose never spoke

American veterans of the Pacific War in WWII occasionally reminisce about 'Tokyo Rose', the seductively voiced siren who broadcast to American forces. Her voice was young and sexy, her message one of surrender, and she told the servicemen that their wives and girlfriends were cheating on them back home. She knew American culture so well she was very likely Japanese-American (one more argument for incarcerating all Japanese-Americans); she did great harm to innocent young men.

Tokyo Rose does sound rather awful, but she didn't actually exist. The servicemen who remember her are suffering from a self-deluding memory (*see also **No one spat at homecoming Vietnam veterans***). There was no such person as 'Tokyo Rose'. There were several Japanese women who spoke on radio broadcasts directed at American forces, but none of them did any more than introduce records. This was actually recognized just after the war. In August 1945, *The New York Times* printed a US Office of War Information announcement that stated: 'There is no Tokyo Rose; the name is strictly a GI invention. Government monitors listening in 24 hours a day have never heard the words 'Tokyo Rose' over a Japanese-controlled Far Eastern Radio.' The woman accused of being Tokyo Rose was indeed a Japanese-American, called Iva Toguri, but she never broadcast anything that could conceivably be held to be demoralizing. In fact, it is claimed that one of her helpers, an Australian POW, cleverly slanted Toguri's broadcasts to give succour to the Allied forces.

Despite all this, in an atmosphere of unreason and intimidation spread by the likes of columnist Walter Winchell, eager to punish traitors, Toguri was indicted and in 1949 became only the seventh person in the history of the USA to be convicted of treason. She was released from jail in 1956, fought US government attempts to deport her, until she was pardoned by President Ford in January 1977 (his last act as president, apparently). Toguri became a Chicago shop-keeper and no doubt served some servicemen who would have sworn (had they known who she was) that the woman behind the counter was the honey-tongued Tokyo Rose who spoke to them in their false memories.

Everyone remembers Tokyo Rose, who never existed, but few now recall the authentically treacherous 'Axis Sally', a Maine woman called Mildred Gillars who broadcast for the Nazis, and was also jailed for treason (she was released in 1959). But as Richard Shenkman, a connoisseur of such cases of selective historical memory points out, Gillars was white, while Toguri was Asian.

There is no proof that anyone burned bras in protest in the 1960s

A ngry feminists burning bras is one of the iconic images of the 1960s and is linked to the demonstrations held at the Miss America Pageant on 7 September 1968. The protest was organized by a group called New York Radical Women. One of the organizers, the poet and novelist Robin Morgan, is said to have told *The New York Times* that bras would be burned in protests outside the venue.

The demonstration was actually preceded by an article in the *New York Post* (not the *Times*) by a sympathetic reporter called Lindsy Van Gelder; Van Gelder said in her article that bras would be burned in a 'Freedom Trash Can' and subsequently claimed that the action was announced in a press release from the protesters. As often happens, it seems to have been a sub-editor on the paper who came up with the catchy term 'bra-burners' and a myth took wing, one enthusiastically adopted not just by reactionaries and cartoonists, but by some feminists themselves. Indeed, some women do seem to have memories of seeing bras being burned, but again, if it did happen, there are no photographs or verifiable reports.

Morgan has denied that there had been a press release advocating bra-burning, but she was quoted in *The New York Times* at the time as saying that she and the other organizers told the worried mayor of Atlantic City that 'we wouldn't do anything dangerous, just a symbolic bra-burning'. A few days after the demo, the *New York Post* carried an excited report of bras, curlers and high-heeled shoes being burned in the 'Freedom Trash Can', though this must have been meant to be satirical. It has also been suggested that the bra-burning saga may in fact have been a hare started in a column by the satirist Art Buchwald, perhaps inspired by male protesters burning their Vietnam draft cards, but it seems certain that Buchwald only entered the fray after the original protest.

Things get murkier still. It has been claimed that some newspapers fuelled the myth by paying young women to burn their bras for photographs, but the evidence for this is lacking. And there is no agreement among feminists as to whether or not it was a good thing even in theory to burn bras, anyway; one wit suggested burning her apron would have been more controversial.

The figure of Robin Morgan herself is now linked forever to the image of burning bras. Morgan can reasonably be described as a prototype for that almost mythical beast, the hardline man-hating American feminist. She has stated: 'I feel that "man-hating" is an honourable and viable political act, that the oppressed have a right to class-hatred against the class that is oppressing them.' A remark that could be said to be of its day, perhaps, but Morgan's rhetoric was characteristically strong: 'Sexism is NOT the fault of women – kill your fathers, not your mothers', and later, in 1972, she was to accuse Ted Hughes of being responsible for the death of Sylvia Plath, an accusation couched in the form of an unforgettable couplet: 'I accuse / Ted Hughes.' ('The Arraignment').

At the beginning of the 1970s, the prime minister could punch you in the stomach in public – and get away with it

We are now so used to the concept of media 'intrusion' that we forget how recently the media has 'intruded' in the affairs and actions of our rulers. In his autobiography, *Strange Places, Questionable People* (1998), the journalist John Simpson recalls how an early assignment found him on a platform at Euston Station with a crowd of other journalists and photographers watching the then prime minister Harold Wilson preparing to board a train. This was May 1970, and Simpson, who had joined the BBC just the previous week, was hungry to make his mark. Wilson stood about, but none of the other journalists approached him. Simpson mustered his courage and walked up to Wilson and began to ask him a question. He managed to say 'Excuse me, prime minister…', then found himself on his back, in pain, staring up at the station roof. Says Simpson: 'It was only five minutes past eleven on my first working day, and I had been physically assaulted by the prime minister.'

So in 1970 the prime minister could assault a journalist in full view of other journalists and photographers and nothing would appear about it in the press, and no photographs would appear either. It would be impossible for this to happen by the end of the decade, with the change perhaps coming around the two hotly contested general elections of 1974. Certain things are still unlikely to be broadcast for a variety of possibly dark reasons. Outbreaks of public violence after football matches in Scotland, for some reason seldom make it into the news, but it is inconceivable – even in Scotland – that a journalist could be flattened by the country's leading politician and it would be kept a secret, that *no one would be expected* to write a report or take a photograph.

John Simpson has a record of rubbing the high and mighty up the wrong way. He has also been hit by Kurt Waldheim (the Austrian president who was apparently the worst-informed member of the Nazi intelligence apparatus in the Balkans), and Osama Bin Laden fumed and wept when he was unable to persuade Afghan mujahedin to murder him, but the 1970 scene he records could not – one hopes – happen today. We live in a more intrusive world, and in some ways, at least, we are the better for it.

Syria may not be run by Muslims...

... And Utah may not be run by Christians. Just as many Christians feel uncomfortable with the Mormons' self-definition as Christians, so numerous Muslims are uncomfortable with the sect that rules Syria. Syria is governed and controlled by an elite from the Alawite minority which declares itself as Shia Muslim, but Alawite beliefs are odd enough for many 'mainstream' Sunni Muslims to consider the Alawites as at best highly heterodox. And although Alawites claim to be Shia, the Iranian theocracy and many (if not most) Shia clerics regard Alawites as heretics.

What makes the Alawites different from other large religious groups (and it is a large group) is that while it is easy to say what Mormons or Unitarians or orthodox Shia believe, it is actually difficult to say exactly what Alawites hold as true faith, as they enjoin secrecy upon their adherents. The publication of doctrine seems to be discouraged and a certain amount of duplicity is encouraged in times of persecution. Thus it is claimed by Islamists that Alawites avoid many practices that orthodox Muslims regard as necessary, and adopt orthodox Muslim customs only when necessary to avoid oppression. Like the Yezidis (who form a large Iraqi minority and do not claim to be Muslim), it seems probable that traditions of secrecy and strategies of deception have enabled the religion to survive. The beliefs of both Alawites and Yezidis may stem from ancient gnostic beliefs. Neither group seems to be keen on converts. It has been claimed that Yezidis worship the devil (they feature a lot in occult fiction thanks to H P Lovecraft, who was fascinated by them), but this is not so.

The Alawite minority took control of Syria by entering the secular pan-Arab Baath party and, perhaps more importantly, gradually securing an iron grip on the armed forces. President Bashar al-Assad could be said to have 'inherited' the position of president after the death of his father, Hafez al-Assad, in 2000. After a 1980 attempt on his life by Sunni fundamentalists, Hafez al-Assad massacred hundreds of Islamist prisoners, and the Sunni town of Hama rose in insurrection in 1982. Assad destroyed the Hama insurrection with appalling ferocity. No one knows how many people were killed in what has been dubbed the 'Hama Massacre' (Amnesty International reckons 10-25,000), but it remains something of a landmark in Middle Eastern repression.

Sunnis make up around 80% of the Syrian population, the remaining groups being a mixture of Alawites, other Shia, Christians, Druze and small Yezidi, Jewish and other populations. The rise of Islamism has led to attacks upon the Alawite minority in Turkey. Alawites are sometimes seen as related to the Alevi in Turkey, a much larger group of heterodox Muslims (with perhaps 20 million adherents, Alevism is possibly the world's least-known large religion). Both faiths suffer persecution throughout the Muslim world, particularly in Saudi Arabia, where all non-Sunni Muslims suffer severe restrictions, including the large Shia minority.

Not in so many words

"A rose by any other name would smell as sweet." This quotable line has undergone some editing – in *Romeo and Juliet*, Juliet's actual words are: "What's in a name? That which we call a rose/By any other word would smell as sweet."

We choose our own ancestors

Ancestry is important to many people, though the sort of ancestry that is important can change over time. Thus Australians used to feel ashamed if they knew they had convict forebears, but now many feel it is a mark of distinction to have convict ancestors, and several agencies specialize in tracing family trees back to those transported to the penal colonies from Britain (and in shading the truth should the crime be truly beyond the pale – a hard-done-by old lag is one thing, but a conviction for bestiality will hardly impress the neighbours). In New Zealand, too, many 'whites' are keen to find Maori ancestors that previous generations might have spurned.

In America, having some Native American ancestry was largely no big deal up until the end of the 18th century. It was not quite the thing for most of the 19th century, and gradually became something of a status symbol in the 20th century. Having some (but not too much) Indian blood came to be seen as making you somehow even more of an American. But it had to be a particular type of Indian to be really impressive, one of the 'civilized' tribes ideally, and preferably the Indian ancestor should be a woman – if at all possible the pretty daughter of a captive. Very rarely, it worked the other way. After making peace with the whites, the Comanche chief Quanah Parker claimed rights as a Texan on the grounds that his mother had been a captive white Texan (which she was, one of the huge Parker clan). Most Texans did not welcome this request, though to be fair to Quanah he stopped his warriors from raping and torturing white captives, doubtless remembering what his father's people had done to his mother's family.

The 'civilized' tribes it was chic to be descended from include Iroquois, Mohawk and Choctaw, but the most favoured is Cherokee. The Cherokee had their own written language and their own newspapers, and were treated badly by the whites, so score all the right points as ancestors. Johnny Cash's biographies and publicity material used to proclaim he had a Cherokee grandparent, but this story was possibly made up for the usual heritage reasons. Other famous Americans of Cherokee descent include Jimi Hendrix, Johnny Depp, Elvis Presley, Demi Moore, Liv Tyler, Kevin Costner and James Brown.

A real fear of many American whites whilst researching their ancestry lies in discovering a black ancestor. In reality, black ancestry must be much more common than supposed (and in Britain also – the black population of Georgian London was larger proportionately than it is today, and many will have intermarried with whites, so their descendants are us). The populist politician Huey 'Kingfish' Long, governor of Louisiana 1928-35, was noted for being an unusual politician in attacking rich people as a class, but remains even more unusual in openly saying that many Louisiana whites must have black ancestry. The smallest bit of black ancestry made you black in the American South: you could pass for white all your life, as in Twain's tale *The Tragedy of Pudd'nhead Wilson*, but once defined as black, you could end up a slave, as the tale's devastating last line makes clear: 'As soon as the Governor understood the case, he pardoned Tom at once, and the creditors sold him down the river.'

The Mythical and the Paranormal

No one has ever been seen to disappear up an Indian rope

The Indian Rope Trick was first described on 8 August 1890 in the *Chicago Daily Tribune*: the 'fakir drew from under his knee a ball of grey twine. Taking the loose end between his teeth, he, with a quick upward motion, tossed the ball into the air. Instead of coming back to him, it kept on going up and up until out of sight and there remained only the long swaying end... [A] boy about six-years-old... walked over to the twine and began climbing up it... the boy disappeared when he had reached a point 30 or 40 ft from the ground... a moment later, the twine disappeared.'

The story was reported as an eyewitness account from American travellers returning from India, but, as the *Tribune* revealed a few months later, it was pure invention from start to finish. But as is so often the way, this full and frank confession did nothing to prevent the story spreading rapidly round the world, gaining fresh testimonies and ever more bizarre variations along the way.

A 'fakir' (from the Arabic *faqir*, a poor man) is a travelling mendicant in India who performs conjuring tricks. The term derives from the Mughal era in India, and seems to have originally been applied to wandering Sufi holy men, but became commonly used for Hindu ascetics also. Fakirs were not universally admired and were seen by some as, at best, charlatans. Indeed, the most bizarre versions of the tale, which have the boy falling back to earth in bits and pieces that the fakir then reassembles and reanimates, sound as if they may even have been fabricated to send up the myth.

The authoritative book on the subject is *The Rise of the Indian Rope Trick* (2004) by Peter Lamont, former president of the Edinburgh Magic Circle. As Lamont's investigation shows, the curious thing is not just that so many people believed in the trick, and claimed to have seen it done, but that so many people felt compelled to find an explanation for an event that never took place.

➤ *See also* **Spoon bending is not necessarily an occult process.**

UFOs have been largely explained

The mystery of UFO sightings has been much discussed since the 1950s, with many books, acres of newsprint, documentaries and movies being produced to meet the demand for information and to feed conjecture. The fact that much of the mystery does not exist any more, that the phenomenon has been in large part explained, and on Britain's Channel 4 to boot, seems to have passed most people by – yet such is very likely the case.

Channel 4's 'UFOs: the Secret Evidence' was broadcast in October 2005, and was presented by a journalist specializing in defence matters, Nick Cook. Cook's thesis is that the 60-year-old UFO 'mystery' is completely explicable. By the end of WWII, military aircraft had developed enormously. In 1939, biplanes still formed at least part of major military airforces; by 1945, jet planes were soaring to new heights and speeds and a new (cold) war had started between the West and the USSR.

Cook argues that the great majority of UFO sightings, from the 'foo-fighters' of WWII (mysterious fireballs encountered by Allied planes over Europe) to the after-pub universe of Scotland's Bonnybridge, can be accounted for by secret flights of secret aircraft. Various intelligence experts were brought on to the documentary to smile in a sinister manner and explain that of course it was all a cover-up, that UFO stories were deliberately planted in order to dupe the USSR. In spite of the protests of ufologists, much of this makes sense. Intelligence agencies had become quite sophisticated at using such tactics by 1945. The British Camouflage Corps was formed in 1916 (the French were first, employing cubist techniques in 1915 to disorientate the enemy), and by the 1940s the British were creating large-scale deceptions using surrealist and cubist artists, and professional magicians also, to create illusions to deceive the enemy.

Other parts of Cook's thesis, in particular his claim that unexplained cattle mutilations may be the result of US military experimentation have been mocked – why not just carry out such experiments at a safe base, at Roswell, for example? – but in truth such behaviour would not be untypical of the well-documented bizarre activities of so-called 'Intelligence' agencies. Much of the true UFO story has doubtless still to be written, but Cook's thesis makes sense – the truth is out there, and it's not little green men we need to worry about.

➤ *See also* **Millions of Americans have not claimed they were abducted by aliens.**

Spoon-bending is not necessarily an occult process

The first major television show to feature a Uri Geller demonstration of bending metal spoons by the power of mind alone was an ITV talk show hosted by Jonathan Dimbleby, in October 1972. Much to Dimbleby's delight, Geller bent spoons live on television and became a celebrity overnight. Next year, Geller tried to repeat his British success on American television, on *The Tonight Show* with Johnny Carson. Carson had been a stage magician earlier in his career, and had brought along his own spoons for Geller to bend. Geller did not succeed in bending the spoons. Carson had been coached by his former stage colleague, James Randi, who subsequently became Geller's most constant and unrelenting opponent.

The abrasiveness of the Randi-Geller interface stems from the fact that Geller feels he is being accused of being a con man, whereas Randi has consistently asserted his belief that people who lay claim to psychic powers can do real damage to the easily persuaded. There have been lots of insults and lawsuits, and commentators walk warily around the issue. Yet the issue of spoon-bending, at least, is a fairly simple one. The charge laid most commonly by stage magicians against Geller is that they can replicate his spoon-bending with no difficulty at all, and they frequently do so. This is not to say, of course, that Geller does not have occult powers. He may do – but the ability to bend spoons does not prove he has them.

A claim by anyone to psychic powers is startling enough, but it is what Uri Geller uses these supposed powers for that many observers find rather disconcerting. The deepest criticism of Geller's claim that he uses occult powers to bend spoons is quite simply the numbing triviality of the activity, given what could be achieved by such powers. It could, of course, be that Geller uses his powers for serious effect 'offstage', as it were, but what cannot be discussed cannot be proven one way or the other.

Geller also once claimed to have made the football in a Scotland v England match move before it was kicked, thus putting the Scottish penalty-taker, Gary McAllister, off his stride (an excuse not previously available to Scottish penalty-takers). Many would also find this intervention into the material world an utterly trivial one, but in any case the true magic happened just after the fluffed penalty when Paul Gascoigne ran up the pitch and scored one of the best goals ever seen in an international; and that feat *can* be convincingly demonstrated.

Millions of Americans have not claimed they were abducted by aliens

A now much-quoted US opinion poll is said to show that close to 4 million Americans think they have been abducted by aliens at some point in their lives. Well, not quite. What the poll certainly does show is that millions of Americans have had 'indicator' experiences which lead the pollsters to conclude that 3.7 million Americans may believe they have been abductees.

As regards those who really do claim to be abductees, the seemingly obvious conclusion, that they are prone to delusion, does not seem to be the case. Such 'abductees' are generally of above-average intelligence, not (despite claims on some sceptic sites) unusually prone to fantasy and display no extraordinary behaviour. Nor are they all Americans. A 1995 study for the University of the West of England, Bristol, found the experience of British abductees to be the same as that of Americans; there are just more of the latter. Nor are all the believers in abductions academically insignificant. The Harvard psychiatrist John Mack came to believe that the abductions were real, and wrote a book about this (*Abductions: Human Encounters with Aliens*, 1994). Mack was killed in 2004 by a drunken driver in London (thus of course fuelling conspiracy theories). The popular British science writer Bryan Appleyard has been criticized for seeming to accept abductee claims at face value in his provocatively titled *Aliens: Why They Are Here* (2004), but perhaps it is just good manners to take expressions of deeply held beliefs seriously.

In 1998 the American magazine *Skeptical Inquirer* published an excellent study of the problem by Dr Susan Blackmore, who suggests that the well-attested phenomenon of 'sleep paralysis' may well provide the answers. Certainly 'sleep paralysis' symptoms are similar to those described by 'abductees': waking up frightened, hearing strange noises and feeling an unwelcome presence, perhaps of something sitting on one's chest. Henry Fuseli's famous 1781 painting *The Nightmare* depicts the experience well. Other explanations, such as suggestions made during therapy and under hypnosis, may also explain some experiences. Dr Blackmore also suggests repeated viewing of television programmes may explain much.

Anal probes (by aliens of humans) often feature in such reports, though, as the alien Kang says to Homer in an episode of *The Simpsons*, it is likely by now that the aliens feel they have 'reached the limit of what rectal probing can teach us'.

Vampires will not get their teeth into all of us

The essence of the vampire problem (in fiction, one hopes) is that vampires seem to want, or even need, to turn their prey into fellow predators. As Van Helsing puts it in Bram Stoker's *Dracula* (1897) 'all that die from the preying of the Un-Dead become themselves Un-Dead, and prey on their kind. And so the circle goes on ever widening, like as the ripples from a stone thrown in the water.' But Van Helsing also tells us (less poetically) that vampires have always been with us. Now even if vampires have the slow digestive capacity of pythons, given the rate of exponential growth that would follow, everyone in the world should have a vampire by now, which indeed is the case in Richard Matheson's fine novel *I am Legend* (1954), where everyone is a vampire except for the hero; the vampires are 'normal' and the hero is a freak.

The true (as it were) situation, as seems to be the case from Mina's coy version of her encounter with Dracula, is that only some victims actually become vampires themselves. The human 'supply side' could therefore presumably last forever. An explanation of what happens when people become vampires is provided in an episode of *Buffy the Vampire Slayer*. Buffy herself (and she should know) gives the details to a still-human vampire 'wannabe', to illustrate the poor logic of such a lifestyle choice. When the vampire 'turns' the victim, the victim's soul moves on and a demon moves in from the 'demand' side of some other dimension. The resulting 'reanimation' is not the original human, but a demon using the body to live in our universe. The vampire may have the personality traits of the original victim – thus the English vampire Spike retains much of the sensibility of a decadent (and déclassé) late Victorian. Spike also illustrates one of the Buffyverse's most striking contributions to vampire lore, in that he undergoes a redemptive process from baddie to goodie, thus indicating that there can be a return journey from vampirism (the other main vampire, Angel, switches from good to bad and back to good – which certainly keeps viewers on their toes).

Some Christian thinkers, such as the 14th-century mystic Julian of Norwich, have suggested that all souls shall be redeemed at the end, as all life is the creation of God and God loves his creation ('every thing has being through the love of God'). If so, far from increasing exponentially, vampirism will presumably have to end in retreat.

The Loch Ness Monster is not a reptile

The Loch Ness Monster is an extremely irritating creature. For a start, 'it' must be more than one, as presumably it reproduces, so if we accept its existence then we have to believe that there is a breeding population in the loch. Common sense dictates that there cannot be an unidentified breeding population of large lake creatures in a modern European country. And most of the famous photographs are either proven or likely fakes, or photographs of wave patterns or floating wood – or deer or otters or something. The photographic evidence is just not there and has not been there since the beast first became a news item in 1933, following construction of the lochside road.

The most irritating thing about the monster is the testimony of people who have seen it. The sightings are frequent and – even allowing for self-delusion – often oddly persuasive. While it seems to be in our nature to be prone to suggestion, we are also wired to recognize a weight of authenticity, and people have been seeing something out there, perhaps since as long ago as AD 565, when St Columba is said to have encountered the creature in the River Ness. The archetype of the superstitious highlander is as annoying as the monster itself, but members of close communities do not willingly present their neighbours with a chance to snigger at them. It seems safe, indeed, to conclude that more locals have seen the 'monster' than have claimed sightings.

The most frequent image people have of the Loch Ness Monster is the classic plesiosaur one – a large 20-30ft reptile with a long neck. In reality (as it were…), this image does not match up with the most credible of the sightings, which tell of something like an upturned boat covered in what looks like elephant hide, a shape that moves like a living animal. And whatever it is, the animal could not be a plesiosaur or related dinosaur. Apart from the fact that large long-necked reptiles would (so to speak) stick out, reptiles of all kinds are air-breathers and have to spend a lot of time out of the water, and have their offspring on land. They also like to warm themselves in the sun, and the sun is almost as mythical along Loch Ness as the monster itself. So whatever it is, it is not a reptile.

So what could it be? Any explanation has to take into account other sightings on other lochs, and indeed other lakes elsewhere in the world, from Okanagan in Canada to Siberia. If there are, as some claim, other universes existing alongside our own, then there may be weak adjoining points at which we catch glimpses from those worlds. Maybe ghosts and monsters are glimpses of these adjoining universes, and perhaps large bodies of water increase the possibility of this happening. Well, perhaps…

Not in so many words

"Suits you, sir!" One of the most successful catchphrases of recent years, this is actually a misquote of what the sublimely horrible pair of slimy tailors say to their customers in *The Fast Show*: "Were you with a lady last night, Sir? Oh, suit you sir!"

Sirens did not have tails

If asked to draw a picture of a siren (as in mythological creature), practically everyone will draw a picture of a mermaid sitting on a rock looking alluring yet a bit creepy, perhaps like the mermaids in Disney's *Peter Pan*. But the sirens were not mermaids: they were sea nymphs who were actually half-woman, half-bird.

Some very striking paintings of flying sirens have survived on ancient Greek amphora – the sirens' encounter with Odysseus being a popular subject. They lived on rocky islands and lured sailors to their deaths by singing their (literally) enchanting songs. In the *Odyssey*, their island is strategically sited near the home of the sea monster Scylla and the whirlpool Charybdis: a rock between two hard places.

There seem never to have been too many sirens, maybe five at most. In early times it was their bird song not their bodies that was seductive, but in classical and Hellenistic art they began to be portrayed as beautiful, and as representatives of the musical arts, even as the daughters of a Muse such as Terpsichore (the muse of lyric and dance). Later still they would be confused with mermaids, which are equally ancient mythical beings (the French word for mermaid is 'sirène').

Odysseus and his crew (advised by the deity Circe) escaped the sirens, as did Jason and the Argonauts (who had Orpheus on board). Jason had been told by the centaur Cheiron that Orpheus would be necessary on the voyage (both Jason and Odysseus knew the value of having high-powered advisers). As the *Argo* approached, Orpheus took out his lyre and simply outsang the sirens. According to some traditions, the sirens drowned themselves if they failed to sink ships, though how they were replaced on the rocks is unclear.

The sirens have inspired artists and writers for millennia. Sir Thomas Browne spoke for many when he wondered 'What song the syrens sang?' in *Hydriotaphia, or Urn Burial* (1658). Fine recent evocations of the sirens can be found in the movie *O Brother, Where Art Thou?* (2000), where it is the later tradition of their physical charms that ensnares George Clooney and his fellow escaped convicts, and in Tim Buckley's 'Song to the Siren', best-known in the haunting Elizabeth Fraser recording.

179

Ugly rumours

Jesus was not a mushroom

In his book *The Sacred Mushroom and the Cross* (1970), the linguist John Allegro put forward the remarkable theory that Judaism and Christianity were originally mystery cults based on the ingesting of hallucinogenic mushrooms. The theory – summed up inevitably by cynics as 'Jesus was a fungi to be with' – was taken seriously by at least some historians and theologians in the early 1970s but it is fair to say that its time has long gone.

Before fixating on mushrooms, Allegro was a highly respected scholar and was part of the team formed to decipher the Dead Sea Scrolls in the mid-1950s. His subsequent book, *The Dead Sea Scrolls* (1956), was a bestseller and established his critical and popular reputation. Allegro was an early representative of a new sort of scholar of the modern age, a presentable authority with one foot in academe, the other in the popular media.

It now seems hard to believe that a book such as *The Sacred Mushroom and the Cross* could both sell and be taken seriously. Allegro said there was no historical figure called Jesus, that the supposed last words on the cross were 'a paean of praise to the god of the mushroom' and when Christians referred to 'Jesus' they were referring to an ancient mushroom god. Further, the figure of 'Jesus Christ' in the New Testament and in early Christian tradition is actually a codename for the red-capped mushroom, *amanita muscaria*, the ingesting of which results in powerful hallucinations. The more Allegro sought to buttress his argument, the worse it got, leading him into very strange places and strange musings for a respected linguist. In all likelihood, it was the sexual ruminations that attracted followers to Allegro as much as the druggy theorizing. In his view, phallism must be central to religion: 'If rain in the desert was the source of life, then moisture from heaven must only be a more abundant kind of spermatozoa.' Charles II said of a preacher popular with nonconformists, 'his nonsense suited their nonsense', and perhaps this is the best verdict on the brief popularity of Allegro's book.

Public flatulence is not good manners in Arabian society

A curious myth persists in Britain and elsewhere that in the Middle East it is good manners to audibly break wind in the course of a meal to show your appreciation of the food. This is not a myth that would long survive actual contact with the process of Middle Eastern dining: farting in front of your hosts is as rude in Tehran and Beirut as it would be in Torquay or Paris, and is no more welcome in restaurants.

The myth is all the more curious as there is a famous short tale in *The Arabian Nights* (*see* **The Arabian Nights were Persian**) called 'The Historic Fart', the story of the unfortunate Abu Hasan. On being summoned at his wedding feast to go and meet his beautiful bride, the bridegroom rises and lets fly a truly monstrous fart. The guests pretend not to notice, but a thoroughly mortified Abu Hasan runs outside, leaps on his horse and rides off into the night. He flees to India and finds service at the court of a 'kafir', presumably Hindu, king. After ten years he becomes homesick and returns to Arabia disguised as a dervish. Approaching the village he fled from, his eyes brim with tears as he beholds his old home and he overhears a young girl asking her mother when she was born. The mother replies: 'The night Abu Hasan farted.' Abu Hasan flees again, never to return.

What is often missed in recounting the tale is that Hasan is actually a Bedouin seeking to move out of his old life by marrying a townie, so the fart has very likely some cultural point relating to social climbing. This also seems to be the case in the *Satyricon* (*see* **Roman houses did not have a room called a vomitorium**), where the crude and incredibly wealthy former slave Trimalchio farts gustily (so to speak) while in company, under the belief that this is good manners in high society. Doubtless similar stories occur in other cultures.

The most famous fart in English history is recounted by John Aubrey in his *Brief Lives* (written near the end of the 17th century), in which he tells how Edward de Vere, Earl of Oxford, farted while being introduced to Queen Elizabeth. Aubrey says the Earl was so shocked he went away for seven years, and on his return, seeing him again, Elizabeth said: 'My Lord, I had forgot the fart'.

It is not, incidentally, a myth that flatulence contributes to the Greenhouse Effect: one estimate has it that around 20% of the world's methane emissions are produced by domestic livestock.

There are indeed few famous Belgians

The old chestnut that there are few famous Belgians is now often immediately followed by the claim that there are actually quite a few; but alas, lists designed to prove the contrary quickly run out of steam. The truth is that there are not many famous Belgians. For a nation of its size, over 10 million, the number of Belgians who have become famous worldwide is startlingly small compared with, say, Scotland, a nation with less than half of Belgium's population.

There is a website that lists hundreds of famous Belgians for the curious – www.famousbelgians.net. There are Hergé and Simenon, of course, but once you get past Magritte, Audrey Hepburn, Jean-Claude Van Damme ('The Muscles from Brussels') and The Singing Nun, you run into a Marks & Spencer chairman, the inventor of asphalt, the inventor of the Body Mass Index and a coachbuilder. The list becomes a list of 'famous' people that few outside of Belgium can possibly have heard of (fictional Belgians, such as Poirot and Tintin, are occasionally sneaked onto some lists to bulk up the numbers). Many supposed French people have of course been actual or arguable Belgians, such as the Paris-born 'rock' star Johnny Hallyday, who sought Belgian nationality in 2006 on the grounds that his papa was Belgian (though some see a tax angle in the identity switch). Hallyday's conversion is annoying to many French sports fans, as his song, 'Tout Le Monde En Bleu', was adopted by the French football team as its anthem during the 2002 World Cup.

If there is confusion over famous Belgians, this perhaps reflects confusion about Belgium itself. The country is seen by fellow Europeans as boring, as the dull heart of the EU, yet it is a strange state that hangs uneasily together. Belgium is a mix of Dutch and French speakers, with a small German-speaking minority. Since 1980 a worthy Court of Arbitration has existed to smooth over cultural and ethnic differences within Belgium, yet these differences are arguably growing, not diminishing. In 2005, Father Damien was chosen as the greatest and most famous Belgian of all time – by the Flemish (the

Dutch speakers). For the Walloons (the French speakers), however, Jacques Brel is the greatest Belgian of all time.

Walter Sickert was not Jack the Ripper

The urge to identify Jack the Ripper is a compelling one for many people. The candidates have included the Duke of Clarence (Queen Victoria's grandson), Sir William Gull (Victoria's doctor), a Polish hairdresser, a Liverpool merchant, an American doctor and an English barrister. It is in fact very easy to link anyone with anybody given the 'six degrees of separation' rule, and in a city such as London during the Ripper murders – five women were killed in the space of a few months in the late summer/autumn of 1888 – it is easy to make connections. It is claimed, for example, that one of the victims, Mary Kelly, had some connection with the Duke of Clarence's household, but even if true this hardly proves that he was a mass murderer. But once an initial (even hypothetical connection) is made, the theorist can then build an edifice that looks completely convincing, but is based on the reader forgetting that conjecture is being built on increasingly shaky conjecture.

In December 2001 the best-selling American crime novelist Patricia Cornwell decided to 'stake her reputation' on her claim that Jack the Ripper was the Victorian painter, Walter Sickert. The suggestion by 'Ripperologists' that Sickert was the killer had been made several times before, but no one prior to Cornwell had been rich enough to buy a series of Sickert works for personal examination, or to spend huge sums on DNA testing of alleged 'Ripper' letters and samples of Sickert's correspondence in search of evidence.

In 1907 Sickert did paint several paintings based on the murder of a prostitute – one is entitled *The Camden Town Murder* (but in fact has the much less dramatic alternative title *What shall we do for the rent?*). They are undoubtedly creepy works but seem to belong (perhaps as pastiche) in the 'problem picture' genre so beloved of 19th-century viewers of paintings: a plausible explanation is that Sickert may have been having a joke at the expense of a no longer fashionable genre.

Could Sickert have committed the 1888 murders? Possibly, but so could many thousands of other men (the time scale is short enough to permit any number of transitory visitors to London to figure). The point is that there is no evidence, only conjecture. Cornwell has found what she claims is DNA evidence that links Sickert with supposedly genuine Jack the Ripper letters (most of the Ripper letters are now believed to be hoaxes anyway), but the case seems very weak according to DNA experts. Given also that Sickert can be shown to have been living in France in the autumn of 1888, the case against him is considerably weakened. Though he could conceivably have scuttled back and forth to do the killings, there remains a complete lack of evidence he did anything of the sort.

Hitler was not a vegetarian

The story that the teetotaller and non-smoker Adolf Hitler was a vegetarian is one of those myths that is almost guaranteed, when questioned, to produce more heat than light. Vegetarians don't like Hitler being one of their company, while omnivores delight in using Hitler as a stick to beat veggies with; it all gets a bit messy.

But while one can reasonably say that 'Hitler was not always a strict vegetarian', the issue is not entirely clear cut. Plenty of people nowadays would confess to being 'vegetarian but with occasional lapses', which seems to be a fair description of Hitler's diet. At the very least Hitler seems to have favoured a vegetarian diet, perhaps because his doctor believed that a meat diet encouraged flatulence (clearly this was not an issue for his vegetarian contemporary George Bernard Shaw, who liked stewed brussels sprouts). He was certainly very interested in animal welfare, and Hitler's legislation banning hunting with hounds is still in force in Germany. His first legislative act was to ban boiling lobsters alive (banning trade unions and other political parties were further down the list).

The Nazis were certainly mixed up when it came to animal rights. Goering loved hunting, and felt Hitler had gone too far, while Hitler and Himmler wanted to go even further in protecting animals. Himmler described the shooting of creatures as 'murder', and his belief that ancient Aryans lived in harmony with animals and the rest of nature certainly had influence within the SS, some of whose members (bizarre though this sounds) seem to have believed quite honestly that they were creating a kinder world.

As with the omnivore attacks on veggies, opponents of animal rights legislation point to Nazi Germany's positive record on animal rights as if this somehow had any bearing on the arguments for better legislation. It could just as well be argued that it is a matter of deep shame that modern Europe still has to catch up with Nazi Germany in respect of legislation against cruelty.

The contradictions in Hitler's position were recognized in his time. He was often described as vegetarian, yet it was widely known that he would occasionally eat ham.

No Japanese department store has a crucified Santa

The belief that there is at least one department store in Japan that displays a crucified Santa at Christmas time is one in a long line of popular stories about Japanese misunderstandings of western culture. Such stories are presumably meant to mock the Japanese for trying to imitate Western culture. One of the earliest stories of this kind described a supposed photograph of a group of Japanese officials wearing western clothes for the first time, getting it right except that they wear the ties over their shoulder (or some such variant). And, of course, to avoid losing face the Japanese have bought up every copy of the photograph – which is no doubt why one can never be produced…

The crucified Santa story works well in popular myth because it combines cultural misunderstanding with the perceived consumerism of the Japanese. In western eyes, the Japanese are often seen as both scary and comic, which, it has to be said, is often how other Asian cultures regard the Japanese. And Japanese consumer society has often taken western traditions and given them twists that don't quite work: an example that may be true is that an organization representing Japanese biscuit manufacturers tried to promote Halloween as a traditional American biscuit festival. Stories of Christmas cards depicting the Virgin Mary on a broomstick can very probably be dismissed, however.

Japan was seen as an all-powerful economic force in the early 1990s. In 1993 the movie of Michael Crichton's paranoid thriller *Rising Sun* depicted a seemingly unstoppable Japanese culture in the process of effortlessly taking over the world. Economists and historians discussed in all seriousness a near-future world in which Japanese economic and cultural power would dominate. It was all nonsense, of course – the Japanese economic model has collapsed and isn't coming back, and neither, it seems, are urban legends about Japanese ignorance of the West, which have simply dried up. So don't expect to hear of any more sightings of crucified Santas.

➤ *See also* **Japan treated prisoners of war very well (in WWI).**

> ### *Not in so many words*
>
> "The Battle of Waterloo was won on the playing fields of Eton." Though attributed to the Duke of Wellington, he never said this. He did poorly at Eton and never had any affection for the place. Nor did he say "Up Guards and at them", just "Stand up, Guards!" He did say in later life that "next to a battle lost, the greatest misery is a battle gained".

No US navy ship challenged a lighthouse to change course

If you use e-mail the odds are that at some point you will receive a 'viral' e-mail containing what purports to be the transcript of a mid or late 1990s dialogue between a US Navy warship and some Canadians (somewhere 'off' Newfoundland). The warship orders the Canadians to change course, but they politely refuse. The Americans reply to the repeated refusals in increasingly brusque, and finally aggressive terms. The transcript generally ends something like this:

Americans: 'THIS IS THE AIRCRAFT CARRIER USS *ABRAHAM LINCOLN*, THE SECOND LARGEST SHIP IN THE UNITED STATES' ATLANTIC FLEET. WE ARE ACCOMPANIED BY THREE DESTROYERS, THREE CRUISERS AND NUMEROUS SUPPORT VESSELS. I DEMAND THAT YOU CHANGE YOUR COURSE 15 DEGREES NORTH. THAT'S ONE-FIVE DEGREES NORTH, OR COUNTERMEASURES WILL BE UNDERTAKEN TO ENSURE THE SAFETY OF THIS SHIP.'

Canadians: 'This is a lighthouse. Your call.'

This is the version of the final challenge quoted by the myth-busting website Snopes, and it includes all the essential elements. The Snopes site is exhaustive on the hoax and traces its origins back to the 1960s (it may go back a lot further, and may even be as old as wireless communication at sea). The myth received a major revival in 1996 and now seems to have found its level as an old friend that pops up in your mailbox from time to time.

What Snopes does not point out is why the hoax story takes this form. It is always an American warship that gets its comeuppance and almost always the Canadians who own the lighthouse (though in Spanish versions it's usually Galicians). The story thus fits into a narrative that mocks the stronger, imperial state and indeed bears a fairly strong family resemblance to the 'Radio Armenia' myths that used to circulate in the days of the USSR. These stories, while pretending to mock the Armenians, very often showed the USSR to a disadvantage, often in a military context, and were quite clever in their subversion of imperial power. The lighthouse story thus functions as a harmless way for dissident Americans to mock their own imperialism (without going down the radical Michael Moore route), and join the rest of the planet in having a laugh at Yankee power. The nationality of the lighthouse can and doubtless will change, but until the world's balance of power shifts, the warship will remain a US vessel (and it will continue to shout in CAPS as in this example).

Charles Manson did not audition for The Monkees

The myth that the multiple murderer Charles Manson auditioned for The Monkees is quite tenacious. The Monkees were a group of actor-musicians formed to play members of a rock group for the eponymous TV show which first aired in September 1966. Over 400 actors auditioned for the parts, including at least two subsequently famous names, Stephen Stills and John Sebastian, but Manson was not one of the 400.

Some of the stories that circulate about the band are true: the mother of Michael Nesmith invented Liquid Paper correction fluid; both Nesmith and Dolenz were quite accomplished musicians; Peter Tork refused to rejoin The Monkees for a McDonald's TV commercial as he is a vegetarian; both Frank Zappa and Tim Buckley appeared on the TV show; and, yes, they made great pop music.

When the TV series ended The Monkees made one of the oddest films ever, *Head* (1968), the cast of which seemingly included anyone who was about, from Zappa and Dennis Hopper to Sonny Liston and Victor Mature. It was written by the then unknown Jack Nicholson, who reportedly described the movie as 'the end of cinema'.

As for Manson, he was a musician and songwriter and can be linked in some way to several musical figures of the 60s – certainly to the Beach Boys through their drummer Dennis Wilson (Manson actually lived with Wilson in 1968). Indeed, Wilson (who drowned off his yacht in 1983 and was apparently the only Beach Boy who actually surfed) recorded a song written by Manson that appears on the Beach Boys album *20/20*. Manson's original lyric was called 'Cease to Exist', but the Beach Boys amended it slightly and called it 'Never Learn Not to Love'. Manson gets no royalties from the song.

The Dalai Lama is not a vegetarian, and does not wear Gucci shoes

A common misconception about the 14th Dalai Lama is that he is a vegetarian. He was indeed a vegetarian for a short period in the 1960s, while living in exile in south India, and addressed the World Vegetarian Congress in November 1967, saying that because there were so many substitutes, there was no reason to eat meat at all. During this veggie period in his life he adopted an extremely odd high-fat diet of nuts and milk and contracted hepatitis B, which resulted in liver damage. Why he should have chosen this odd diet in preference to the glorious cuisine of south India (though in large part milk-based, this food is both vegetarian and very healthy) remains a mystery.

The Dalai Lama was persuaded by his doctor to eat meat – in moderation – for 'health reasons'. He apparently eats meat every other day, and at a French state dinner in 1998 where he was a guest of Chirac, he refused the vegetarian option and ate the calf's cheek, saying 'I'm a Tibetan monk, not a vegetarian'. Tibetans do commonly eat meat, as the climate of Tibet is unsuitable for most crops. And many Buddhists throughout the world, while they may follow the

Buddha's guidance not to kill living things, will accept meat provided by another (there is much debate about this among Buddhists).

Rupert Murdoch famously described the Dalai Lama thus: 'I have heard cynics who say he's a very political old monk shuffling around in Gucci shoes.' This comes from an interview in the October 1999 issue of *Vanity Fair* and appears to imply that the Dalai Lama is a bit of a hypocrite with a taste for luxury goods such as ludicrously expensive Gucci shoes. However, even those sceptical about the western search for beneficent eastern figures to venerate recognize the Dalai Lama's simple lifestyle. The main flaw people find in him is a certain naivety, but given what he has had to endure from his enemies and even from supposed sympathizers – the American TV host Larry King once introduced him as the world's leading Muslim – he can surely be forgiven. He may not be a vegetarian, but he has no Gucci shoes, literal or metaphorical.

Adelaide is not the murder capital of the world

This is one of those myths that has a satisfyingly precise origin. On 18 July 2002 a documentary on Channel 4 described Adelaide as 'the murder capital of the world'. As is the way, the description keeps resurfacing, but is not true. As the Australian newspaper *The Age* pointed out, Adelaide is not even the murder capital of Australia, and compares very favourably to major cities elsewhere. The murder rate is less than London's and much less than that of Pretoria and Washington DC.

Adelaide City Council is understandably outraged at this slur on the 'City of Churches' (as it prefers to be known), and the ongoing damage to 'Brand Adelaide'. And yet, there is a twist to the Adelaide murder myth. Although the murder rate is nowhere near as high as many cities, there have been several spectacular slayings in the city and its suburbs, most notably the so-called 'Snowtown Murders' or 'Bodies in Barrels Murders' of 1999. Eight dismembered bodies were found hidden in plastic barrels in the town of Snowtown, north of Adelaide, and two more bodies were subsequently found buried in an Adelaide back yard. The victims had been tortured before they died, and one was partially eaten by the killers. Much of the detail of the case remains suppressed.

The Channel 4 'murder capital' documentary was on the disappearance of British backpacker Peter Falconio. Falconio's body has never been found, and in December 2005 an Adelaide resident, Bradley John Murdoch, was convicted of his murder. The British media covered the story in huge detail and the relationship between Falconio and his fiancée, Joanne Lees, came under much scrutiny. But what the British media largely missed in its coverage of the story was that the Australian police investigating the disappearance inferred immediately they were involved in a murder case, as the scenario of a drifter picking up victims is not an unknown one in the Outback – or in Adelaide, for that matter.

Religion

The animals did not go in two by two

This gets complicated, so pay attention. Here are the relevant instructions from Jehovah to Noah in Genesis:

'Of every clean beast thou shalt take to thee by sevens, the male and his female: and of beasts that are not clean by two, the male and his female... Of clean beasts, and of beasts that are not clean, and of fowls, and of every thing that creepeth upon the earth, there went in two and two unto Noah into the ark, the male and the female, as God had commanded Noah.'

So there were seven of each 'clean' beast; verse 7.9 demonstrates (as several creationist websites show) that these seven went into the ark as three pairs of each species plus a spare (presumably in case something went wrong with one of the pairs). It can perhaps be assumed that the 'unclean' or filthy beasts could be relied on to reproduce, and maybe in the end it didn't really matter with the lower sort of creature.

Most creationists are certain that dinosaurs were on the ark, though it seems unclear whether they were clean or not; it depends on whether the definition given by Jehovah to Moses and Aaron applies in this case or is redundant. It seems possibly not: two brachiosaurs must take up a lot of space, seven would be just silly (one creationist site speculates that only very young dinosaurs got on board).

Sceptic sites, as one would expect, take the mickey out of the Flood story. The ark's dimensions – calculated by one creationist as 450 feet long, 75 feet wide and 45 feet deep – just don't seem big enough for a literal interpretation of the text: Noah would have struggled getting around 50,000 species on board, plus over a million insects, plus all the food.

People who try to find the remains of the ark call themselves 'arkeologists' and at least one TV documentary has been made on arkeology at Mount Ararat in Turkey, where creationists believe the ark finally came to rest.

Medieval theologians had no interest in angels dancing on the head of a pin

Though often cited as an example of medieval obscurantism, there is actually no evidence whatsoever that any medieval scholar or theologian ever wasted any time in calculating how many angels could fit (or dance) on the head of a pin. There is a passage in Book 1 of Thomas Aquinas's *Summa Theologica* (written c. 1266-73) where Aquinas raises the question of whether a number of angels can be in the same place at the same time. In fact, Aquinas did not believe that angels occupy physical space, and only raises the question to dismiss it. Aquinas's supposition that angels could travel without passing through space is now a fairly standard device for science-fiction writers. The concept of the so-called 'wormhole' through which spaceships pass in order to get from one galaxy to another might have been a travel solution at least as comprehensible to medieval scholastics as it is to contemporary SF fans.

Aquinas on angels has been misrepresented by both anti-Catholic and anti-scholastic scholars. The earliest 'pin' reference seems to be in the preface to the Anglican divine William Chillingworth's *Religion of Protestants a Safe Way to Salvation* (1638), which defends Protestants against the charge that they have no tradition of learning to compare to Catholic scholasticism: 'As if forsooth, because they dispute not eternally… Whether a Million of Angels may not sit upon a needles point? Because they fill not their brains with notions that signify nothing, to the utter extermination of all reason and common sence, and spend not an Age in weaving and un-weaving subtile cobwebs, fitter to catch flyes then Souls.'

Some Anglican divines (including Archbishop of Canterbury William Laud) were notably uneasy about Chillingworth's assault on scholasticism but eventually let it be published. It was another Anglican, the Neoplatonist Henry More, who got the angels dancing in his *The Immortality of the Soul* (1659): 'those inconceivable and ridiculous fancies of the [medieval] Schools; that first rashly take away all Extension from Spirits, whether Soules or Angels, and then dispute how many of them booted and spur'd may dance on a needles point at once'.

Millennial expectations of faith groups are always confounded (so far, at least...)

The early Christians believed that Christ would return soon – the 'Second Coming' due any time. Eventually, as Christianity became established and Christians took over temporal responsibilities and rewards, these expectations dissipated, though they would re-emerge in times of crisis. It was perhaps natural to assume, as in times of plague, that if disaster has overtaken you, your family, and everyone you know, then Christ must be due. Similarly, the fact that the Christian Apocalypse has been forecast many times and has not yet happened is not discouraging for believers, as it is the believer's involvement in the experience that is all-important.

There are generally four main events now expected in fundamentalist Christian eschatology: Christ's Second Coming, which will bring a 1,000-year rule of peace; the Tribulation, when Antichrist will rule; the Battle of Armageddon, which Antichrist will provoke; the Rapture, when the born-again will be lifted into heaven by God. The sequence in which this will all happen is not entirely agreed, however. The hugely successful *Left Behind* series of novels begins with the Rapture and ends with Christ's victory over the Antichrist (the concept of the 'Rapture' is actually quite recent, emerging in the 19th century). The state of Israel is especially important to many American millenarians as that is where Armageddon will be fought and where some Jews will be converted to Christianity (the rest are damned).

Notions of terminal decay and an imminent end long predate the beginnings of Christianity. There is apparently an Assyrian clay tablet from around 2800 BC which laments the corruption of the present time and the coming final days, and in the 7th century BC, many Romans expected their world to end. The significance of 1,000-year cycles in Christianity derives from the first significant monotheist religion, Zoroastrianism, but the process of calculating the actual dates has proved to be anything but an exact science within Christian eschatology, so the last days are always coming up for somebody.

Muslim expectations of the end of time seem to have increased in modern times, especially among those Shia who believe the 12th Imam, who has been hidden by God since AD 868 will be revealed soon. Iran's President Ahmadinejad is reported to believe that the main function of his country's 1979 Revolution was to pave the way for the imminent return of the 12th Imam and Judgement Day.

Not in so many words

"The reports of my death are greatly exaggerated." In 1897 a reporter heard that Mark Twain was at death's door in London, and called on him to check. It was actually Twain's cousin who was ill, and Twain told the reporter that "The report of my death was an exaggeration." Twain later "improved" the story by adding "greatly" (and there was never a wire sent to a London paper, as the anecdote commonly has it).

Darwin did not convert to Christianity on his deathbed

Adherents of all major proselytising religions are fond of repeating stories of deathbed conversions; the more prominent the convert the better, and even better if he or she has been a famous non-believer. Charles Darwin would have been a good capture for evangelical Christians and perhaps it was inevitable that a conversion story would emerge (though many Christians do not see a clash between faith and evolution; *see* **There is no scientific ferment over intelligent design**). The story about Darwin's deathbed conversion was spread by one Lady Hope, who claimed, in a speech at the evangelist Dwight Moody's school in Massachusetts, that she had visited Darwin on his deathbed, where he had repented of propounding the theory of evolution, and that he wanted her to gather a congregation where he could 'speak to them of Christ Jesus and His salvation'.

It is often claimed that Lady Hope herself was fictitious, the invention of American evangelists, but she was real enough, the second wife of Admiral Sir James Hope. The Darwin family was outraged at the claim. Henrietta, Darwin's daughter, said in *The Christian*, 23 February 1922, that Lady Hope was not present at any period of Darwin's illness and she was certainly not present at his deathbed, and added: 'He never recanted any of his scientific views, either then or earlier. We think the story of his conversion was fabricated in the USA.' As her brother Francis Darwin said in his biography of their father, Darwin was an agnostic, not an atheist, and there was no deathbed conversion to theism.

In the modern Middle East it has become common for reports to spread of the deathbed conversions to Islam of prominent Arab secularists and Christians, a notable example being the founder of Baathism, Michel Aflaq. Aflaq's supposed conversion or 'reversion' (it is common in Islam to call converts 'reverts') was proclaimed by the professedly secular Iraqi government in 1989, but the truth of this claim remains highly disputed.

There is no scientific ferment over intelligent design

The concept of intelligent design (ID) arose in the late 20th century, and its main proponent is a conservative Christian think tank in Seattle called the Discovery Institute. The Institute promotes ID as an explanation for the origin of life: life is said to be too complex to have evolved according to Darwin's theory of evolution, and therefore there must be a 'designer'. The literature on the subject is growing, and has been fuelled by US creationists attempts to get ID accepted as a theory of human origin that is at least the intellectual equal to the theory of evolution. The Discovery Institute has adopted a 'fair play' tactic in the USA, suggesting that it is only 'fair' that ID be taught in schools along with Darwinism, and there have been some clever attempts at balancing the two theories. Thus it is sometimes argued that not all proponents of ID take comfort from the fact that George W Bush (and the Christian Right) supports the cause. And not all Darwinists are overjoyed by belligerent counterattacks on theism.

Yet on the central issue of proof there is no debate within the scientific community. ID is simply not taken seriously at all by the vast majority of scientists, who regard Darwin's theory of evolution as a cornerstone of modern science. The consensus of science is that Darwin got it right with *On the Origin of Species by Means of Natural Selection* (1859), and the developments in life sciences since his time have added to his case, not weakened it.

As at least one Roman Catholic theologian has pointed out, it is forgotten by many supporters of ID that the theory of evolution does not actually deny the existence of God (*see **Darwin did not convert to Christianity on his deathbed***). It is a curious fact that the majority of 19th-century Christians and other theists made a quick (and largely painless) accommodation with Darwin, yet this is a move many 21st-century Christians in the USA still seem unable to make. Opinion polls indicate that only one in four Americans believe that life has evolved through natural selection, and that around half of all Americans believe the earth is only a few thousand years old.

It seems generally assumed on the ID side that the creator is benevolent. The counter to this has already been made most tellingly by Darwin himself – that he could not reconcile the existence of a benign creator with the life cycles of parasitic wasps. The response to this by theologians is often humane and carefully weighted, but the position of modern creationists seems to be simply that the world and its works are for man: the apparent suffering we see in nature is a result of our misunderstanding. At its most extreme, this view leads to the position that we are meant by God to use the world and its resources and there is no need to bother ourselves with such annoying questions as global warming and the finite nature of energy sources – as one senior American politician has put it, Jesus is coming soon anyway. ·

➤ *See **Millennial expectations of faith groups are always confounded (so far, at least...)**.*